I TRIED TO LOVE THEM ALL

THEM ALL

The Story of My Six Marriages

I Tried to Love Them All

Them All

The Story of My Six Marriages

Joanna Fuller

As told to

Margialee Schlachter

ISBN 13: 978-1507742327
ISBN 10: 1507742320
Ebook ISBN: 978-0-988773677

Acknowledgments:

Cover Art by Mary Lee Wilkinson
Cover Art © by Mary Lee Wilkinson 2014
Cover Design by Marilyn Neilans

G J Publishing
515 Cimarron Circle, Ste 323, Loudon TN 37774
865-458-1355
www.neilans.com
booksbyneilans@aol.com

PROLOGUE

One night as we were about to sit down to dinner, with the food cooking on the stove, we heard Dad's truck roar into the driveway. It took him several minutes to get out of the truck, and his uneven footsteps on the porch were audible signs that he'd been out drinking again.

When Dad came through the door he bumped into the door casing. Swaying as he walked in, he said, "What's that awful smell? Don't tell me we're having that same slop you made night before last!"

Mom replied, "About time you showed up. Whatever it is you'll eat it!"

Dad stepped back and backhanded her across the face. "Talk to me like that, will you, woman?" He said.

Mom put her hands up to her face and found her nose was bleeding. When she saw the blood she went wild with rage. "You sorry drunken son of a bitch," she shouted. She grabbed the handle of the skillet on the stove and flung its contents at him. As soon as the hot food landed on him he was hooting and hollering and trying to get his hands on her again.

"You bitch," he shouted. Before Dad could corner Mom she made a mad dash for the back door and crossed the road to Aunt Clara and Uncle Roy's, where she spent the night.

Dad shouted to me, "Get me a towel!" I ran to the stove and grabbed a dish towel and threw it at him. He wiped his face and hands and proceeded to remove his overalls, shirt and shoes. "That bitch will pay for this," he said. "I work damn hard to keep food on this table for all of you and this is the way she treats me when I get home! I should kick her ass out of the house for good!"

Dad said to me "Clean up this mess," as he grabbed his clothing and shoes and headed for the laundry room.

Once he'd left the room I said to Karen, my little sister, "I'll make peanut butter and jelly sandwiches for us when I get this food off the floor."

When Dad came back through the kitchen he grabbed a beer from the refrigerator and headed upstairs to his bedroom.

Karen and I ate our sandwiches with glasses of milk. Then I cleaned the table and we went to bed. I was twelve years old and my sister Karen was five when this happened.

Here is my life's story.

CHAPTER 1

My name is Johanna Kay Fuller. I was born March 22nd, 1940 to Maxwell and Mimi Fuller and was raised on a farm in Holbrook, Wisconsin, a small farming town with three stop lights and a population of less than ten thousand people. Dairy farming was the source of income for most of the farmers. My Dad drove a milk route picking up the farmer's milk in the mornings and taking it for processing to the milk plant.

As I take you along on this story telling journey of my life, you might enjoy reading about it, but you sure as hell wouldn't have wanted to live it.

I've had six marriages and five divorces. I was widowed once. I've gone from last name Fuller to Robinson, Beard, Montgomery, Dawson, Kennedy, Foster, and back to my maiden name Fuller. I plan to remain a Fuller for the rest of my life.

In the morning after the food fight, Mom waited until she saw Dad's truck pull out of the driveway before she returned to the house. I was making toast to go with a glass of orange juice. Karen was still asleep upstairs when Mom entered the kitchen. I ran to her and we hugged each other.

"Mom," I begged, "Why don't we just leave here? Can't we go live with Aunt Trudy or any of your other sisters? They've all asked us to stay with them."

Mom replied, "I've thought about it, believe me, Jo, but I'm so scared of your dad. He'll continue to make my life miserable even if I do get away from him. He'll drum up some excuse to have you girls taken away from me. He'll find a way to be the good guy and make me out as the bad parent. I couldn't bear to have that happen. I'd rather be dead. I'll go to Aunt Hilda's today and have another talk with her. I can't live like this anymore."

When she got home, Mom told me about her conversation with her sister. Aunt Hilda had said, "When you see the condition Max is in, can't you try counting to twenty and not making matters worse by arguing with him or talking back? Also, Mimi, your taking up drinking in the afternoons isn't helping either. You're in no condition to use good judgment. Please, for the sake of the girls, try zoning out by counting to twenty and walking away if you can. Maxwell isn't going to change his ways; it will have to be you who does the changing and who will be the better person. Think about what this bickering is doing to your daughters. It's bad enough that they'll never know what a loving father/daughter relationship should be."

Mom had said, "You're right, Sis. I'll really work on holding my tongue. How could I have picked such a loser as a mate? I love my girls and will do whatever it takes to keep us together until they are grown."

Only later did I realize why Mom wouldn't leave Dad. She had been truly afraid she'd lose us.

In our home the focus was on my parents' addictions rather than the needs of us kids. Because we didn't know what to do, we were consumed by a feeling of helplessness. My sister and I both experienced jitters and stomach aches throughout our formative years. The unpredictable behavior of our parents caused us chronic stress, which we learned to adapt to with denial and repression.

When I look back now I see a lot of Mom's mistakes repeated in my own life. We both just wanted to be loved and cherished.

CHAPTER 2

Mom came from a large family. Her mother, Ruby, died after giving birth to her seventh child. Mom's dad, Melvin Gibson, didn't know what to do with all the kids. He decided to adopt out the two year old boy, Glen, and the newborn baby girl, Connie Jo.

Melvin married Elizabeth Goodman a couple years later. She was good to the five older children. It was years later, when the girls were all adults, before they were reunited with their two younger siblings.

My dad came from a large family too. He was always the son out of step, so to speak. Back then they called him the *"Black Sheep"* of the family. None of my uncles - Walt, Cecil or Roy - treated their wives the way Dad mistreated Mom. It wasn't like Dad got away with beating up on Mom all the time. Many times she was just spoiling for a good knock down fight. She was getting his attention … but it was the worst kind.

Back in the 1940's, women weren't as career minded as they are today. Then, most women just wanted to get married, settle down and raise a family. A future as a wife and mother was their picture of happiness in life. Marriage was what they longed for and dreamed about. Once my mother graduated from high school she had no future plans to advance her education.

Mom's four older sisters - Hilda, Beverly, Trudy and Sara - were all very attractive, and Mom was too. They all had beautiful curly black hair. Mom and Hilda had high cheek bones and dark eyes. They were all tall and had great figures. But Mom was always working on her looks to make herself stand out and be noticed.

She had insecurities and my dad played off them. Mom was very jealous. Dad was a huge flirt with the ladies and didn't try to control his behavior; therefore, it was the cause for many of their arguments. I should say their fights because once an argument got started Mom kept it going until things were flying, and the two of them got physically into the hair pulling and shoving each other around the house. She couldn't give in, and if he was drinking at the time the battle was ten times worse. Neither of them ever actually won a fight, because it exhausted both of them.

I'm sorry to say it, but Mom began to drink to dull her pain and their relationship went further downhill from then on. Family members tried to intervene, encouraging my folks to get family counseling but they didn't do it. It wasn't a safe atmosphere for us girls. We never knew when we came home from school what to expect. I couldn't have friends over very often because my parents would start fighting in front of them.

The only relief we had from this drama was when our Grandpa and Grandma Fuller would come and get us for a week-end or when we stayed with them during the summer when school was out. We looked forward to visiting them as they didn't scream and shout at each other but treated us with kindness and love. They knew we had it rough living with two angry and abusive parents.

Granddad said to my dad "Why can't you treat Mimi better and show her some respect?"

Dad would just say "I've tried, Dad, really I have, but she is so explosive and has such a temper it doesn't work."

Granddad knew that his son was weak and was retreating into alcohol to escape. He told Dad, "If I ever hear that you've put your hands on either of those girls I'll see to it that you rot in jail!" He made that sentiment very clear over the years.

I always knew that we could go to my grandparents or my Aunt Clara and Uncle Roy's for safety if we needed to run away.

My life as a parent/mother developed at the age of twelve. I took it upon myself to keep my little sister safe. I braided her hair, told her to pick up her toys, to wash her hands before meals, and a lot of little things that my mother should have been doing. When Mom started drinking in the afternoons before Dad got home from work she simply forgot how to be a good mom.

Being a twelve year old kid I didn't know what I could do about Mom's drinking, but I tried to talk to her about it. She'd just listen quietly then say, "Try not to worry, Jo, I'll do better."

I knew it was a lot of hot air and lip service but I'd shut up and let the conversation drop.

I denied for years any anger in being placed in this helpless position at my young age; however, years later when I faced up to the facts, I realized that I had taken on the role of mother to Karen, and that I truly resented being thrust into that position by my own mother.

My folks played cards with five other couples once a month. When it was Mom and Dad's turn to host the gathering at our house Mom would clean the house from top to bottom, making snacks and setting up a drink bar on the kitchen counter. She was the hostess with the cute little apron and the whole bit on those nights. My folks were trying to present themselves as the perfect happily married couple. Sister Karen and I were always sent upstairs and were not to be seen or heard from for the rest of the night for any reason.

One Saturday night when I was twelve years old our lives changed in a moment of madness. My folks came in from a night out drinking at a local bar. Dad walked the sitter out to the porch and waited there until she'd crossed the road and turned off her porch light. During that four or five minutes Mom, who was drunk and mad, got my Dad's deer rifle down from the closet shelf. She put a cartridge in the chamber and bending over the gun, pulled the trigger. BOOM!!!

I awoke when I heard the loud noise, and started down the stairs. Dad told me to get back upstairs and to stay there. I heard him call the sheriff and then he called Aunt Clara who lived across the street. She was at our front door in a matter of minutes. She came upstairs and circled me in her arms.

Aunt Clara said, "I want you to grab a pillowcase and put a change of clothes in it for your sister and yourself. You both are coming home with me." I did as I was told - not knowing that I would never see my mother alive again.

I remember waking up early at my Aunt Clara's house the next morning. I was only a kid and I was hopeful that Mom was just wounded.

Aunt Clara came into the room and said, "Let's go downstairs so we can talk without waking Karen." We went downstairs to the family room. My aunt got each of us a glass of orange juice from the refrigerator and we nestled together on the couch.

She knew what she had to tell me would be tough so she started out by saying "You know, Jo, your Uncle Roy and I love you two girls as if you were our own children. We'll always be here for the both of you. Last night should not have happened. Your mom went too far and it breaks my heart to have to tell you … she's dead."

I sat there numb, hearing the words and trying to clear my mind. How could Mom do this to all of us? I began to sob and my aunt gathered me in her arms and rocked me back and forth. I cried and cried; we both did, over the loss of my mom.

When I quieted down and my tears stopped flowing, Aunt Clara said, "I'm going to ask a huge favor of you, Jo. You've been like a second mother to Karen, and now she will need you to hold her close so we can all get through this."

I knew she was right. I could and would continue to help raise my younger sister.

CHAPTER 3

Years later I heard my mom's sister Trudy talking about the night Mom killed herself. She said the kitchen looked like a war zone with parts of Mom's body splattered all over it. I'm glad I didn't have to witness that. I don't think she knew what she was doing at that moment. How could she leave us? I was her first born and her favorite. She had told me that she would love me forever. It was a lot to handle and I still cry just thinking how she left this world and all of us.

After a few days at Aunt Clara's, when the funeral service was over, we returned home. I had a difficult time going into the kitchen. Dad asked me to fix him a sandwich. I froze, in a helpless state of anxiety. I felt a sensation of numbness and just couldn't go in there. I called Aunt Clara and she came over. She became the buffer, a protective shield, standing between me and the memory of what had happened to my mom in that kitchen. She slowly talked me into choosing my own spot from which to work.

"Put out of your mind where your Mom stood or how she did things. You establish a pattern of your own. One that works for you, Jo. I'll help you work through this," she said.

We managed together and I began to function in the kitchen. My dad thought I could just take over the household duties without outside help. I was only a twelve year old kid and it was all I could do to get a meal on the table and keep the laundry done. I was overwhelmed with all that was being heaped upon my shoulders. Aunt Clara came over every week to help me change the bedding and to write a grocery list for Dad when he shopped in town. One day as we were changing the sheets on Dad's bed, Aunt Clara decided to flip the mattress. When we lifted it up, we saw a book lying on Mom's side. I picked it up and looked at it. Mom's handwriting was on the cover. It was *her diary.*

"You take that book into your room and put it in a safe place," Aunt Clara said. "I'm sure you'll have a better understanding of your mother's life when you read what she wrote about what she went through being married to your dad. She wouldn't have wanted so much work of keeping this house and your younger siblings heaped upon you at this young age. Try to remember, Jo, she loved you kids with all her heart."

Aunt Clara cared so much for us and was always there for me. I don't know what I'd have done without my loving, wonderful Aunt Clara.

CHAPTER 4

My dad stayed sober for several months after Mom's closed-casket funeral. I did a lot of caring for my sister. She was only five years old and she could remember some of the sweet things about Mom, which was a blessing. Being older, I remembered a lot of stuff I wish I could forget.

I didn't read Mom's diary right away, but I finally took it out from under my mattress one night and was shocked to learn that I wasn't Mom's first child. She'd had a stillborn baby boy a year before I came along. When she was in her first trimester carrying him, Dad had been drinking and knocked her down the porch steps one night. He didn't take her to the doctor as nothing appeared to be broken. The stillborn baby had a deformed skull. She was convinced that the fall from the porch steps had probably caused the deformity. Then, a couple years after I was born, Mom had a miscarriage and lost another baby. She didn't hint of any abuse from Dad in the diary about this pregnancy.

Mom expressed her grief over the loss of these babies because she wanted children so badly. As I read the lines she'd written, I could tell my mother had been through hell with my dad. He really was the *black sheep* of his family. My heart ached as I read the story of her life with my father. The words written on the pages of her diary were blurred from the tears she'd shed while writing them. She had tried so hard to please him and to make the marriage work.

She wrote about the night I had the lead in the school play in fifth grade. She'd reminded Dad that morning to try to be home early so we could have supper and then go to see me perform.

When he didn't show up and it was time to leave she called Aunt Clara to see if she would drive us to school. Aunt Clara picked us up and we got to the school on time. Mom wrote that her heart broke for me because I wanted my dad to see me in the play. I'd rehearsed my part for weeks.

When the play was over Aunt Clara drove us back home. She kept telling me what a great job I did and that I didn't look nervous up there on stage at all. When we got home Mom asked Aunt Clara if she could borrow her car. She wanted to go looking for Dad. She asked if Aunt Clara would stay with us girls for just a little while and that she wouldn't be gone long.

Mom knew which bar Dad hung out in and drove right to it. His pickup truck was parked in the lot but he wasn't in the bar. She took a seat and ordered a soda. She was looking out the window and could see his truck. She waited, knowing he'd have to return to it sometime. Before long he opened the door on the passenger side of the truck and stepped out zipping up his pants. A young little redhead with a real short skirt hopped out of the truck and draped herself on him as they made their way back inside the bar. When he stepped inside Mom met him at the door. "I see this is your choice to hang with tonight instead of attending your daughter's school play. What a worthless excuse of a father you turned out to be!" She looked at the young girl and said "You're young enough to be his daughter - and speaking of daughters, he has two wonderful girls at home this very minute, one of which is probably crying her eyes out because her dad didn't care enough to attend her school play."

Mom turned on her heels and headed for the door. She left the bar and returned home. She wrote in the diary that she felt so helpless that night that if she'd had a gun she would have shot Dad - not between the eyes but between the legs!

Aunt Clara didn't have a thing to say when Mom returned. What could she say? She'd seen many of these situations over the years between Mom and Dad and knew she couldn't do anything to change it. Dad was going to do what he wanted when he wanted no matter how much it hurt Mom's feelings.

I read her diary over and over even though it brought me sadness and tears. The light had gone out in my mother's eyes because of Dad's treatment of her, and I remembered how quiet and withdrawn she had become.

Halfway through her book I found a snapshot of Mom and her four sisters, Trudy, Sara, Hilda, and Beverly. They were in their teens and all looked so beautiful and happy together with wide smiles upon their faces. I want to remember Mom like that: young, vibrant, smiling, and full of life.

I found it difficult to show any respect towards Dad after reading her diary. I went through the motions of not showing disrespect but my feelings were smoldering inside. I vowed that never in my life would I let a man put me through what my Mom had gone through with my dad.

CHAPTER 5

I'll never forget my first car ride with a boy. It was when I was almost sixteen years old. My girlfriend Sally and I were at school one night for band practice when two boys that she knew asked us if we wanted a ride home. I thought that it would be okay, plus it would save Sally's dad from having to come pick us up. She and Dave got into the front as it was Dave's car and Sam and I got into the back. The car had just started up when Sam was all over me, touching my breasts and groping me between my legs.

I told him, "Cut that out!" But he wasn't hearing anything I said. He just laughed and continued to push me down and plopped himself on top of me. I was furious with him. He tried to kiss me and I bit him on the lip. He sat up, then hauled off and slapped me on the side of the head. I saw stars for a moment; then I kneed him in the groin. I was satisfied to hear him groan in pain.

I yelled, "Stop this damn car!" Dave stopped the car, then got out, and moved the seat forward so I could get out. It was pitch dark that night and it took me a few minutes to realize that we were only about a mile from my house. They all wanted me to get back into the car but I wasn't having any more of Sam pawing at me, and I headed off on foot.

I let Sam know the next day at school that if he ever tried anything like that again he'd get more of the same from me. Also if he ever said anything bad about me to his friends, that I'd have my dad come over to his house and work him over.

I think that first experience with a boy set the standard bar high for me. I'd seen enough rough stuff at home, and I knew that I'd never let a man lay his hands on me against my will.

I might mention now that with all that fighting at home, I learned a lot of cuss words. I picked up on it and throughout my school years it got me into a lot of trouble. My mother talked like a drunken sailor as well as my dad. Before I knew it cursing had become my way of expressing myself when provoked.

CHAPTER 6

When I turned seventeen, I was finally relieved of my role as mother to Karen. Dad began seeing a widow lady, Dana Zimmerman, whose husband had died a couple years earlier. She owned a dairy farm on his milk route, and that's how they met. She was a nice pleasant woman, and welcomed Karen and me into her lovely farm home.

I got to pick which bedroom I wanted on the second floor. I happily chose the back bedroom because it had a lot of windows that overlooked the meadow. I could see the animals out there in the pasture lying down in the sun, and the dogs sleeping outside the fences. There is just something about being on a farm that seems like you are living close to nature. I loved the tranquility in my new home.

Dana treated us like we were her own daughters. I could finally be myself and enjoy my senior year in school without all the stress and worry of keeping house and looking after my sister.

Karen took a bedroom at the front of the house. It was larger and she could put her dolls and all her collectibles in the large closets. She was ten and she needed a mother, like Dana, to guide her through her upcoming teen years.

After we got all moved into Dana's place, Dad sold our farm. Our farm held a lot of bad memories for me, which I was ready to let go of, but I missed seeing my Uncle Roy and Aunt Clara. They had been extended family to Karen and me for a lot of years when we really needed some sanity and stability in our young lives.

CHAPTER 7

When school was out I found a job working for Wilson's, a Manufacturing Company. They handled car parts, and I worked as an office clerk and secretary. I liked the work and the people on the job.

My responsibilities included taking orders over the phone and at the front desk. I processed the orders into the system by using the typewriter. I had taken typing in school and could type more words per minute than were required for the job. I liked meeting the public and my eight hours went flying by.

I even had time to help some of the other workers finish up their duties every day. My boss finally told me that it wasn't necessary for me to do their work for them. He said that he'd been watching how some of them handled their workload and they wasted their time knowing that I'd step up and help out. He wanted to see if they could do their own jobs in an eight hour period.

I understood what he was saying, and after our conversation I started straightening up the stock room at the end of the day instead of doing the other employees' work for them.

CHAPTER 8

I had my eye on a fellow, Tony Robinson, who lived in a neighboring town. He was so shy. One night, some friends introduced us, and Tony said, "Would you like to go to the drag races with me this Friday night?"

I was attracted to his dark eyes and his shy smile. I was happy that he'd asked me out on a date. I said, "I'd love to."

We dated a lot in the following weeks and then Tony suddenly said, "Jo, will you marry me?"

I was on cloud nine. I thought marriage to Tony was going to bring me the happiness I wished for. I really wanted to be a wife and mother, not a career woman. But I soon realized that I'd married a lazy Momma's Boy. He worked only when he felt like it. His job was in a car repair garage that his father owned. I soon found that If Tony didn't feel like getting up in the morning on any given day he'd just stay in bed.

I figured things out fast regarding our incomes. I'd be the one working steady to pay the bills, rent, car payment, and insurance; I'd be the one running the household.

So much for the shy, cute guy I had been crazy about a few months back. He was now the beer-bellied, hung-over, lazy good for nothing nightmare I'd married. I kept my mouth shut, and continued to go to work every day. What other choice did I have at this point in my life?

I soon found myself pregnant. *Momma, where are you when I need you?*

After our son Eric was born, I had someone to love. He was such a sweet baby, and I hated to leave him all day at day care while I worked.

Virgil, Tony's dad, let him off the hook as far as showing up for work on a regular basis. He always let him slide, as far as his responsibilities were concerned. I think Virgil gave Tony money, even when he missed work. At any rate, I didn't see much of his paycheck. My money went for most of our bills. We fought over the day care bill, and I insisted that Tony pay that one out of his paycheck. I had hoped that even if he wasn't a good husband that he'd at least try to be a good father and love our son, but Tony loved his life as a spoiled brat and just wouldn't grow up.

When I was coming to grips with this chapter in my life, I knew I was too young to handle it. We had many arguments about Tony not taking responsibility for a wife and child. When our arguments got heated, he'd just walk out; leaving for a few hours was his way of dealing with all his problems.

I sat at home a lot of nights pacing the floor, crying my eyes out, trying to find a way to get out of the mess I'd made of my life. I thought of going to Aunt Hilda but knew what she'd have to say, *"You made your bed - now lie in it."*

Tony wanted to continue going out with his friends. What *I* wanted didn't matter. We continued to fight and then, *Whammy*, I found out I was pregnant again! Now I knew how my mother had felt in her marriage *trapped*! I needed psychotherapy for sure.

My love turned to anger and hate towards Tony. He wasn't going to change his lifestyle for me and our babies, no matter how much I begged and pleaded.

One night, when Tony did come right home after work, I made a good dinner and we played with the boys before baths and bedtime. When I got them down for the night, I said, "I'd like to ask you a question and I want a true answer. Please tell me why you asked me to marry you so soon after just six weeks of dating?"

Tony thought about it for a minute and said, "Well, it was because you wouldn't have sex with me, and I was hurting, and needed for you to show me that you wanted me in your life."

There, so that was it: not that he planned for a long future together, just that he wanted *sex*, and I hadn't been putting out. I said, "Thank you for being honest with me." Now I knew I'd have to get myself out of this dead end marriage with a boy who didn't want to become a man and own up to his responsibilities for a family. Tony had always been given everything he wanted, when he wanted it, and that included me. How could I have been so *stupid*! I now found myself on the same road my mother had traveled and would have to find my own way out of this mess I'd made for myself.

Once I wrapped my head around my situation I stopped trying to make it better. I decided I would bide my time, have my second son, Kent, and then get out of this marriage. It would just take a little planning on my part.

I'd been saving a little money. There was a coffee can on the top kitchen shelf, and I'd put a five or ten dollar bill into it whenever I could. I told myself that when my stash reached four hundred dollars, I'd go see an attorney and get a life for myself and my sons.

One day after work, I had a ten dollar bill to add to my savings. I got the coffee can down and was horrified to find it *empty*! That sorry son of a bitch had *stolen* my money! I waited that night for Tony to come home from work and I flew into a *rage* when he walked into the apartment. I lit into him with both hands. I called him a no good, lazy excuse of a man, "and a *thief* at that!"

I grabbed my purse and car keys and told him, "You're in charge until I get back." I drove like a *crazy* person but soon realized that if I *killed* myself my sons wouldn't have a loving parent to raise them; so I calmed down and headed to my father in-law's garage.

I marched in and shouted to Virgil that I wanted to talk to him in his office. He wiped his hands on a rag and followed me to the back of the shop.

I closed the door and told him "That sorry excuse of a son of yours *stole my money* that I've been saving in a coffee can."

He listened until I'd finished talking, and then quietly asked, "How much did he take from you?" I told him four hundred dollars. He opened the cash register and handed me five one hundred dollar bills.

I said, "Thank you." I walked out and went back to the apartment. Tony was asleep on the couch with the TV blaring. I shut it off and went to bed. I would call a lawyer the next day on my lunch hour, and set up an appointment for the following day, to start divorce procedures.

The next night when Tony didn't come home from work, I got a suitcase down out of the closet, gathered up all his clothes, and began throwing them into it. I set it outside on the front porch.

After a long hot shower, I crawled into bed, exhausted. My marriage was over!

When I went to court to obtain my divorce, the judge ordered Tony to pay two hundred dollars a month for child support, which was to go for day care. He didn't want to do it, but his father made sure that money was sent to the courts every month.

After my divorce was final, Tony hardly ever came to see his sons. He didn't care to take them for more than a few hours at a time, and the visits usually ended up with Tony dropping the kids off at his parent's house while he partied with his buddies.

I was barely speaking to Tony after the divorce but I did tell him, "I'll make sure that your folks are part of our son's lives because I know they adore the children. Eric and Kent may well be *the only grandchildren* they'll ever have. I want them to have the kind of relationship that I had as a kid, with my Grandpa and Grandma Fuller."

I wanted to find someone to love me, and to love my sons. The more men I dated, the more desperate I became. I hooked up with a bunch of losers, always trying to take care of them or mother them. After a while, I realized that seeing somebody new and trying so hard to make them perfect just wasn't working for me. I was expecting too much from a relationship, perhaps more than any man could give. Still, I felt I needed a mate, someone to come home to at the end of the day.

"Looking for love in all the wrong places," like the words to a great country song ... that was me.

CHAPTER 9

My sister, Karen, was now sixteen and came by to play with her nephews on the week-ends quite often. The boys loved her and she was so good to them. I said to her, "Karen, I can tell that when you become a mommy you will be a loving parent."

I'd stayed in touch with my girlfriend from high school, Sally Todd, and a good friend from work, Vicky Adams. They would come by on some Saturdays, so we could visit, and they would play with my sons.

Sally got on the subject of my dating again. "You need to get out there and give yourself a chance to meet someone new," she said. "Moping around the house won't change a thing in your life."

I knew she was right, and I did join them a couple times at a local dance club, but always felt guilty leaving the boys with a sitter after they'd already been in day care five days a week.

I was having a hard time making my paycheck stretch to cover all our expenses. Even with Tony taking care of the day care bill I still had the rent, car payment, insurances and food to pay for.

I went to my ex-mother-in-law, Maude, and asked her if she would be willing to look after the boys so I could work on Friday and Saturday nights. Then I could work a part-time job for a few months, to get a little money ahead for emergencies.

Eric was four and Kent was three, and they could be a handful at times, but she agreed to try it.

I started looking for some kind of work that fit into that time frame. My friend Vicky said, "Ralph's Pub is looking for a bartender on Friday and Saturday nights. Do you think you could handle that kind of a job?" I'd never even mixed a drink but I was willing to learn. Whatever it took to make some extra money I was willing to tackle it. I was so tired of always being in debt.

I walked into Ralph's Pub and asked to speak with the owner.

A tall good looking fellow extended his hand and said, "Hi, I'm Bud Beard the owner ... and you are?"

"I'm Johanna Fuller," I said, "and hopefully your new bartender."

"So ... you're looking for a job. Have you ever done this kind of work before?"

"No, but I'm a fast learner," I replied. Bud smiled at me through the most beautiful blue eyes I'd ever seen.

He laughed. "I'll tell you what, here is an application. Take it home and fill it out. I'll give you a list of mixed drinks and how to make them. You study it and come back on Friday night at seven. My bartender, Leo, is leaving in two weeks and he will show you the routine. If you can handle that plus the rowdies that hang out in here you're hired." We shook hands and I walked out of there feeling good about the chance to prove myself.

All that week during my lunch hour, my friends quizzed me on the mixed drinks until I'd practically memorized the list. I could and would ace this job!

Friday night was a rush for me. After I got off work at five, I picked up the boys from day care, and stopped at McDonald's to pick up dinner for the three of us. When we got the food home, I put it on the table, and while they were eating, I changed my clothes and shoes, washed my face and reapplied my makeup. After finding a pair of good working shoes, we were back in the car and on our way to Grandma's house. That morning before I went to work I'd packed them each a change of clothes for the next day. I told them to be good for Grandma and kissed them and held them tight for a moment.

I arrived at the Pub at seven sharp. Bud met me at the door.

"Wow, do you look great," he said. "I think you'll sure brighten up this place. Now, if you can make drinks, you're in." His blue eyes seemed to stare right through me, and I was very attracted to him.

I thought to myself, *where have you been all my life?* Then I told myself, *Slow down, girl. You've got a job to do here and if you want to stick around a while you'd better be damn good at it*. I handed Bud my application and he handed me an apron. He showed me a locker for my purse, and then we walked behind the bar to meet Leo.

"Hi girl," he said. "So you're the new hire!"

"That's me, and I plan to stick around for a long time," I said.

Bud said, "Show her the ropes." Leo took me to the walk-in cooler and explained how they filled the well with beer. He showed me where the extra liquor was stored and how to record for inventory when you removed a bottle from that area. It didn't seem too difficult to me.

"Thanks Leo," I said. "I think I can handle it."

The bar started filling up about nine o'clock. I was running up and down the length of it to fill customer's orders. I managed to keep up and joke with the patrons, too. I have a good memory, and was even able to say to some of the regulars, "How about another beer … Budweiser, wasn't it?"

Leo kept telling me that I was doing a great job. "You're a natural at this bartending gig."

I was so glad to be complimented.

I stayed busy cleaning bar glasses whenever the customers were all taken care of. The time passed by quickly and as the regulars began leaving around closing time I was on a first name basis with a lot of them. The regular customers treated me with a lot of respect and welcomed me to the job. I appreciated that kind of response and was glad to be a part of the group. I needed a little fun in my life.

Leo said as he wiped down the bar after the last customer left at two o'clock in the morning, "Kid, you handled this job like a pro. Bud's found himself a new bartender!"

I said, "Thanks Leo, I learned from a pro. You're so good at your job; you made it easy and fun for me."

I counted up my tips and had over fifty dollars for one night's work, plus my hourly wage! I gathered up my purse from my locker and headed for my car. "See you tomorrow night, Leo."

When I got home I walked out of my shoes, threw off my clothes, and fell into bed exhausted. I even forgot to wash off my makeup; I was so ready for sleep. When I looked at the clock beside the bed the next morning, it was eleven o'clock. I jumped out of bed anxiously, and then remembered that the boys were over at Maude's. The house seemed too quiet without them. I phoned

Maude to see if she wanted to go to lunch with the kids and me.

Maude said, "I have a hair appointment at 12:30 today."

"Then I'll just pick up the boys and take them the rest of the day. I'll be over in a few minutes."

I drove over, picked up Eric and Kent, and took them to Dairy Queen for lunch. As I sat there watching them eat, I thought to myself how lucky I was to have them. Money was tight for us, but somehow we'd make it. Memories of Bud crept into my thoughts as I watched the kids play. Later when I was doing laundry at home he came into my mind again. Maybe he was married with kids. *I'd better concentrate on my part time job at the pub and forget about hooking up with Bud.* If working the second job was what it took for awhile, I could do it.

My sons came first in my life. They were so young and really needed me. Kent's little hands on my face at night when I tucked him into bed warmed my heart, and Eric's last request for a story to be read to him; that was what kept me going.

CHAPTER 10

That evening I bathed the boys and fed them. While they played with their toys, I got ready to go to work at the pub.

Karen called. "What's up, Sis?" she asked.

"Well, I've taken a part time job working on Friday and Saturday nights at Ralph's Pub as a bartender."

"You've got to be kidding me," she said. "What do you know about serving drinks?"

"Last night was my first night. I managed just fine. I even made fifty dollars in tips."

"Who's watching Eric and Kent for you?"

"They're staying overnight with Grandma Maude. She seems to be enjoying her grandsons."

"Good for you Sis. If you ever get in a pinch for a sitter, you can count on me to help out with the boys."

"Thank you, Karen; I've got to drop them off now. Stop by whenever you can."

I walked into Ralph's at seven and headed for my locker. I grabbed my apron and put away my purse.

Leo walked up and said, "Sure good to see you back, girl."

"Can I ask you something, Leo?"

"You sure can. What is it?"

"Well, I was just wondering about Bud. Is he married ... or going with someone?"

"Interesting that you're asking about Bud. He was married for ten years but his wife left him. He has raised his only daughter, Tracy, by himself. She's now sixteen and a sweet kid. Bud is a good dad. He has dated over the years, but never got serious about anybody. Funny you should inquire about him because he asked me about you last night."

"Oh, really?" I said. "What did you tell him?"

"I only said what you told me, about being divorced and raising two young boys on your own."

"Thanks for the info, Leo." I said, and then turned back and asked, "Is Bud here tonight?"

"He'll be in later. Tracy is in the school play this year and tonight he'll be with her until ten P.M."

I got behind the bar and started serving the customers. The time flew by. I looked up and Bud walked in. He was smiling at me. His blue eyes just twinkled.

"Good to see you, Jo. How's it going?" he asked.

I said, "Just fine. Busy as usual."

"I can see that you're able to handle it. I'll be back in the office working on some papers."

Around midnight when the crowd was thinning out I said to Leo, "I think I'll take a five minute break, if it's ok with you?"

Leo said, "That's fine. Why don't you go see what Bud's doing?"

"That's just where I'm headed; are you a mind reader?"

"No, but I can see the way the two of you look at one another."

"Just keep that information to yourself, Leo. I don't want to be the gossip at the bar, when there really isn't any story to tell."

Leo said, "I got it."

I opened the office door and found Bud cleaning off his desk "Hi, Boss. I'm just taking a five minute break now that the evening is winding down."

"How did things go out there tonight?" Bud asked.

"I'm getting more relaxed working the bar and I'm getting to know the regulars by their first names."

"That's good because if the regulars like you, that's where the tips come from." Bud continued, "Not to change the subject, but Leo tells me you're the mother of two young sons. Tell me about them."

"Eric is four and Kent is three and they can be a handful at times. I have to leave them in day care five days a week. I work to make a living for all of us, and value the time that I do spend with them. They stay overnight with their grandmother on Friday and Saturday nights while I'm working here at the pub."

"I'd like to meet them sometime. Maybe we could all go to the park some Sunday afternoon. I have a border collie named Billy who happens to love kids. Do you have any plans for tomorrow afternoon; let's say around two o'clock?"

Bud was asking to take all of us to the park.

"I haven't anything planned for Sunday. The boys love the park," I added.

"I have your address from your application, so it's set: I'll pick you all up tomorrow."

"I'd better get back out to the bar and help Leo clean up." I was feeling so wonderful, and glad that Bud wanted to spend some time with me and my boys.

Leo told me, "I can handle this till closing, Jo. You can knock off early. Go home and get some rest."

"Are you sure, Leo?"

"Go on, get out of here."

I took off my apron, gathered my tips and purse, and left the bar. When I got home I counted my tips and had even more than the first night: sixty dollars! This was the best job, and I was starting to build a nice nest egg for emergencies.

The next morning, I picked up the boys from Grandma's house and took them home. While they were eating breakfast and watching cartoons on TV, I told them that my new boss had asked us all to go to the park that afternoon. He would bring his dog, Billy, so they could run and play with him. Eric loved dogs and asked if he could take a disk to throw for the collie. I said, "Good idea, but we'll ask Bud first if it'll be okay."

Bud picked us up at two o'clock sharp. He had Billy in the truck with him, and as soon as he stepped on the porch, the boys were out the door. I called, "Boys, wait up, let me introduce you to Bud first, then we'll go play with Billy." Bud laughed at me, because he could see how excited they were to meet his dog.

We piled into the truck and were on our way. The boys were so happy to be going to the park.

Billy loved the boys and the attention they were giving him. Bud just sat on the grass and watched them running and playing together. He laughed out loud at the fun they were having. Bud had a lot of patience with my boys. It was so relaxing to be with a man who obviously enjoyed life. He loved my kids from *Hello*!

Bud kept looking at me out of the corner of his eye. I noticed, but didn't say a word. I was so attracted to him, but I promised myself I'd let him do the courting. If anything happened between us, I wanted it to be him taking the lead. It didn't take long before he said, "I don't want to scare you off, but I have to tell you how attracted I am to you. You have such a zest for life, an upbeat attitude, and a laugh that just draws me to you."

I was speechless for a minute. I finally found my voice and replied, "Well, since we are being honest and truthful, Bud, I get butterflies when I see you coming at me, looking at me through those beautiful blue eyes."

Bud said, "When the boys get tired out and Billy has had enough running around, we'll take him home, and feed him. Then, if you can get your sister to watch the boys, you and I will go out to dinner. How does that sound to you?"

"I'd love that, Bud."

I called Karen from the pay phone on the corner, to see if she could sit for a few hours, and she agreed.

"I'll meet you at your place at five thirty. "Sure, I'd love to spend a few hours with the kids. I'll feed them, bathe them, and read to them before bedtime. You two have a wonderful dinner. I can't wait to meet this dude. He sounds like a keeper."

After Bud got Billy home and fed, we left his house and as we returned to mine I saw Karen's car in the driveway. She ran out to embrace the boys. As I introduced her to Bud, I could see by her actions that she was pleased to see what a nice fellow I'd met.

Bud selected a little Chinese restaurant in town. He ordered our dinner and while we waited he took my hand in his and said, "I want to get to know you better, Jo. I haven't felt like a school boy in a long, long time. I hope I don't scare you off by being so forward and blunt about my feelings."

"You don't know how happy I am to hear you say the wonderful things you've said to me, Bud. I'm a direct and straight forward kind of person, and I appreciate your honesty with your feelings. We've both been hurt by our past relationships. If we take this slow and get to really know each other, I have good vibes for us in our future."

I felt so protected and safe with him.

CHAPTER 11

We began to make room in our lives for each other. Our work schedules were very busy, and as we became closer as a couple Bud and I talked about the future. He wanted me to get into something I really enjoyed, and I told him that I'd always wanted to sell real estate. He suggested that we set some goals and strive to achieve them. With his encouragement I began taking a real estate class on Monday nights.

Over the next six months, we were together every day, somehow, for at least a few hours. I was dog tired with not enough hours in the day or night to get everything done. Bud finally suggested, since I'd completed the course in real estate, that I should start looking for a job in that field. It only took me two weeks until I had a job offer at a local office. I gave my notice at work, and since I now had quite a nice little savings account built up, Bud found someone to take over the bartending job at the pub. He was so happy now that I wasn't so stressed out and overworked.

His daughter, Tracy, and my sister, Karen, had met at school, and they became good friends. Tracy was taking college courses during her junior and senior year. She was college bound, and Bud was so proud of her. Karen wasn't interested in going on to school. She had a boyfriend, Junior Cline, and would probably get a job after graduation, but only until they married. We all got along great as a family. My sons now had an extended family and they loved all the attention from everyone.

Eric was in school, and Kent was going to pre-school, and they were both much happier. Each boy had his own little personality. Bud loved them as if they were his own. Those who didn't know that he wasn't their biological father saw Bud as a very loving and caring dad. I could not have asked for a better man to be added to our family unit.

The holidays were coming up soon, and Bud enjoyed decorating his house and yard. He had a lovely home and took such good care of it.

One night, we were lying on the couch at my apartment when he suggested, "Why don't we get married? We could make it a holiday wedding."

I knew we had been getting close to making this kind of commitment and I just reached up and gave him a long kiss and held him in my arms. That was my answer to his question.

Bud said, "I have more free time than you do, so I'll run around and get some prices so we can decide just what we both want for food, decorations, etc. You can pick out the invitations and make up the guest list."

I knew this marriage was the correct decision for me. Bud was the kindest, most giving person I'd ever met. He truly loved me and my boys.

When we told Tracy and Karen of our plans to have a holiday wedding, they were thrilled for us. I sent out fifty invitations to families and friends. We decorated trees in the yard and the house was lit up so beautifully.

Our wedding day was December 22, 1964. Bud was just beaming as he spoke his vows. I can't remember ever being happier in my life. Surrounded by family and friends, all pleased that we'd found each other, we enjoyed a beautiful ceremony.

We left that evening on a three day honeymoon to the Bahamas. Tracy and Karen were left with the boys. I felt comfortable with the two of them in charge at home. They would all have a great time together celebrating Christmas.

Bud and I went to a resort where he taught me to play golf, which I loved. We took long walks, holding hands and learning a lot more about each other. We were so in love as we made plans to grow old together. The three days passed by too quickly and we found ourselves back at the house.

I returned to my real estate job and Bud went back to working days at the pub. Things were going along well. We went to church on Sunday mornings and played in the yard with the dog, Billy, most Sunday afternoons. Bud and the boys adored Billy.

Bud and I golfed with a group of friends on Saturday mornings. It was good exercise for both of us, and a nice way to socialize.

I think this time in our lives was the happiest for all of us.

CHAPTER 12

On our first anniversary we went back to the Bahamas for a few days. It was a second honeymoon for us. We were a good match and our love for each other was as strong as the day we married. We both worked at keeping our love a priority. I'd never had such a good man who cared for my happiness like Bud did.

The boys were getting older and doing well in school. Bud showed them so much love as a father. He would often say, "I am so lucky to have found Jo and her boys."

We worked and played together and our lives were filled with much joy and laughter. It seemed like nothing could change that.

But it did. Bud woke up one morning and said, "I'm having a hard time getting my breath this morning."

I asked, "Do you want me to call the doctor?"

"Yes, I think I'd better have it checked out," he answered.

I called the doctor, and he wanted Bud to come in at ten o'clock. I offered to go along, but Bud said, "You don't need to, Honey, I'll be okay."

The doctor ran some x-rays and told Bud he didn't like what he saw. Bud had a mass on his right lung. The doctor wanted to take a sample of the mass and have it tested. Bud explained to me, "I'll be all right, try not to worry."

He'd never been a smoker but working in the bar he was around smoke all day. We continued to worry and when the doctor called it was the worst news.

Bud answered the phone call from Doctor Green. "Bud, I hate to have to tell you this, but you have cancer and it's in an advanced stage." I saw the color drain from Bud's face as he learned the news. It was what we had dreaded and we were devastated.

I called Karen, to keep her informed about Bud's health. She loved Bud, and was just crushed to hear the news.

Over the next two months we tried to keep things as normal as possible, but it was hard not to think about Bud's health and our future. We began making changes in our lives with this dreadful news. Bud got a day manager for the bar and worked from home, paying the bills and keeping up with the operation of the pub. I knew he missed seeing the patrons and good friends he'd made working the bar over the years.

Bud had his good and bad days. He wasn't a complainer and he tried his best to be in good spirits for all of us. I worked from home as often as I could so that I could be nearby if he needed me. Sometimes at night I'd cry for all of us and the hell that Bud was going through with this illness. We were in it together, and he was thankful for the time he still had to spend with the family. His daughter Tracy had been told about his illness right from the beginning, and she phoned often from college. If you've ever been in this position, you know it's hard on everyone.

On the day Bud passed away, January 9th, 1969, his daughter Tracy was with us, by his bedside. We said our goodbyes. He slipped away in peaceful sleep and was gone. We couldn't wish him back to suffer that again.

We had Bud cremated and sprinkled his ashes over the lake near his boyhood home.

We had had nearly five great years together. I'd been blessed to have had him in my life. He was a wonderful father to Eric and Kent and they missed him dearly.

When Bud's will was read a month later, we found that he had provided well for us. The beautiful house was ours. He'd set up Tracy's future by taking care of all her college expenses. He left the bar to her and had good management in place until she could run it, or manage it, herself. Bud had selected good people whom he trusted to look after his affairs.

CHAPTER 13

For the next two years life seemed so empty for me. I went through the motions of daily living, but I felt lifeless.

I concentrated on my job and my sons once again. They were growing up fast. Eric began having some problems in school. It wasn't because he couldn't do his class assignments; he just failed to turn them in on time. He just didn't seem to care if he did well or not. Kent had an easier time in school, but I could see trouble coming down the road. He wanted to do as his older brother did, and Eric didn't take direction well.

One day my sister called and asked, "What are you doing this Saturday night?"

"Why, what do you have up your sleeve?"

"Well, Junior has a friend, Spencer Montgomery, coming over tonight and I thought maybe we could all play Poker. I hate sitting here listening to them talk about the good ol' days. Do you think you could help a sister out for one night?"

"I don't get to see you enough these days, that's for sure. I'll look forward to it. What time should I be there?"

"Come over whenever you want, Sis. Spencer will be coming around seven o'clock."

"I'll be there before seven. See you Saturday night."

When I met Spencer I wasn't interested in finding romance or hooking up with him. I was still in mourning over the loss of Bud. Spencer seemed like a nice enough fellow. We laughed a lot and I had a good time playing cards that night. Spencer wasn't pushy, but I could tell he liked me. He had a good sense of humor and a quick wit. He was a good friend of Karen's husband, Junior. They talked me into going golfing with them the next Saturday. I loved golf and hadn't been out on the course since before Bud got sick.

We continued to get together for cards, and after several months, Spencer said, "Tell me, Jo, do I have a chance in the future with you?"

I liked him; he was a nice guy. I replied, "I'll tell you the truth, Spencer. I don't like being alone. I've applied for a government job. It will probably be a couple years before I can get a position. If you can put up with the possibility of my relocating to a new city, we'll face whatever happens at that time."

Spencer pulled me into his arms, and kissed me. It felt good to be wanted and needed once again.

I didn't feel comfortable bringing a new man into the house that Bud left us. I put the house up for sale and it sold in two weeks. We'd had a lot of wonderful memories there that I would keep in my heart forever.

On November 6th, 1972, Spencer and I had a quiet wedding ceremony at the chapel on the college grounds. Our attendants were Karen and Junior. I didn't want any fanfare, and Spencer agreed with my wishes.

I found a townhouse to lease close to my job in town. The kids didn't have to change schools so their lives didn't change all that much. Spencer sold restaurant equipment for a living and had to travel four or five days a week. With him gone so much of the time he wasn't there to help me with the boys. They were at an age where they didn't want to do as Momma said. I felt pushed to the limit at times, and I found myself unable to handle them. I'd get so frustrated when they acted out or misbehaved. I couldn't be the good parent as I knew I should have been. No one said that raising children would be easy. I later realized they had been missing Bud, the only loving dad they'd ever known.

We'd only been married a year when I received a letter from the Federal Government. I'd been offered a job in Pasadena, California. I'd been working on getting a government position for years and finally, it was going to happen. When Spencer got in off the road I handed him the letter. He read it and I could tell by his reaction that he wasn't happy. He'd lived his whole life in Holbrook, Wisconsin. Relocating wasn't something that he wanted to do. We sat down that week-end and finally came to a decision. I'd follow my dream and he'd continue living in Holbrook. The marriage would be over. He'd only invested one year into it and I guess it didn't mean enough for him to try to salvage it. I reminded him that I'd made it clear about this job when he asked me to marry him. I felt that since he traveled on his job what difference would it make where he lived, but he didn't see it that way.

I wanted to take this position, with or without Spencer. I phoned the number supplied in the letter and accepted the offer. I had one month to get out west and get settled. I called a storage business in Pasadena and had my furniture and personal items shipped there. But first, Spencer moved into an apartment of his own and started the procedures for divorce. Meanwhile, I gave a week's notice at work. I got out of our lease on the town house and packed the car for our trip across the country.

Karen did not want me to move so far away from her. She asked, "What will I do with you so far away?"

I said, "You'll do like most other people do, you'll pick up the telephone and call me to stay in touch; and I'll do the same."

By now, Karen had two children. Her boy, Bradley, was three and her daughter, Sissy, was eight months. She was a stay at home mom and was wonderful with her kids. Junior supported his family by operating his own car repair business, and he was doing well financially. It seemed to me she had the perfect marriage.

The boys didn't give me any grief over the move. I think they both wanted a new adventure in life. They were thinking of warmer weather out west. I notified their school and picked up their records.

My boys and I loaded the car and were soon on the road. We stopped at points of interest and really enjoyed the adventure.

CHAPTER 14

When I reached Pasadena in January, 1973, I found an apartment in the area of my new job. The kid's school was only four blocks away, and they could walk to it every day. I called the storage company and set up a time for delivery of our furniture.

I took the boys' school records over to the school. They were all enrolled for classes and would start the next day. I busied myself getting things set up and purchasing whatever I needed. I still had a week to find my way around this city before I started the new job.

Things were working out as I had planned. I didn't have time to dwell on my short, one year marriage, or the end of it. Some things just don't work out as planned, and I accepted that. I was starting a new life and it revolved around me and my boys once again.

I knew I'd made the right decision in coming out west. Bud had made sure that I was provided for financially. I was determined to use my money wisely so that I'd never be dependent on a man for support. I could make my own living. I was willing to work hard to get ahead in life. I was following Bud's advice, setting goals and working toward them. I'd learned early on that I could be successful in my career even when my personal life was in serious disarray.

The first month in California, the boys did well in school. I soon realized, however, that Eric seemed to be drawn to kids who needed help. He brought a couple of them over to the house. Their lack of manners and their slangy way of talking didn't make me very pleased with his choice of friends.

I looked into finding a Big Brother's program so my sons would have positive role models. This worked for Kent, but Eric was a loner, and didn't want to continue in the program, so he dropped out.

Granddad Fuller called me out of the blue one day and told me that my dad had died of liver failure. "Grandpa, I don't know what to say."

"He had abused his body with booze for years so it wasn't much of a surprise that his liver failed him." Grandpa said.

"Still, it must be hard to lose a son no matter what the circumstances. My thoughts will be with all of the family," I said, and hung up the phone.

I had made up my mind long ago that whenever my dad passed, I'd not be attending his funeral. After reading Mom's diary and knowing how mean he was to her, I didn't have an ounce of respect for him. I truly felt he had driven her to her death.

I called my sister. "Hi, Karen, I just learned from Grandpa about Dad. I'm not coming back for his funeral. Please don't try to talk me into it."

"It's your decision and I respect it. I've heard from Mom's sisters and none of them are planning to attend the funeral either. I'll go, though, and sit with Uncle Roy and Aunt Clara."

On the day of the funeral, I took Mom's diary out in the alley and burned it in a barrel. That was the end to Mom and Dad's miserable life as far as I was concerned. I couldn't let it consume me any longer and I needed to move on with my own life.

On the positive side, I loved my new government job. I'd finally been accepted in a position that gave me a lot of responsibility. I knew I could handle the work load, and I thrived on it. The recognition that others valued my skills was endlessly affirming. A new job, new apartment, new friends; I was ready for all of it.

I worked in several interesting departments, and was often sent out on consignment to sub-contracted positions. I felt accepted on my job. My boss, Warren Taylor, trusted me to take responsibility and to complete my assignments on time. He never had to prod me to finish a manual and I had no problem getting up in front of a room of people and explaining my projects.

The first five years I learned so much about how the government operates. As I moved up the ranks in department positions, I got the feeling of acceptance. Many promotions came my way. I wrote manuals on "How to operate and manage certain aspects of the job." A lot of my work was confidential, which gave me a lot of satisfaction. I finally felt that I amounted to something. I'd arrived as a trustworthy individual, ready to play ball with the big boys.

The only cloud on my horizon was my older son, who was in and out of trouble the next few years. The school principal called me about him on a weekly basis. I could see that Eric was headed for serious trouble, maybe even jail. Finally when he reached seventeen, he announced one morning that he wanted to join the army. He was a big boy and looked older than his age. I signed for him to join the service.

He did not contact me for many years after he joined. I lost touch with him. Even though I tried over the years to find Eric, I couldn't locate him. I didn't know at that point if he was dead or alive.

My younger son Kent stayed in school, but he too, just drifted through, going just enough to receive his diploma. After he graduated I found that he was staying in bed until after I left for work every day. This had to stop. One Saturday morning I knocked on his bedroom door and said, "Kent, I want to talk to you out in the kitchen." No answer. I knocked again and this time, I opened his bedroom door.

He said, "Close the door, I'm not ready to get up yet!"

I walked over to the foot of his bed, lifted his mattress, and slid it half off the frame. Kent was wide awake now.

"Ma, what the hell do you think you're doing?" he said.

"I'll tell you what I'm doing. When I asked you nicely to come to the kitchen so we could talk you ignored me. Well, since I'm putting the roof over your head, and the food on your table, I think you could show me a *little* respect. If you think for one moment that you'll be staying here, continuing to live off me, you'd better think again. You're free days are over now that school is out. You'd better get out there and find yourself a job. You decide; join the service, as your brother did, or go to work and support yourself." I walked out of his bedroom. He now had something to think about.

The rest of the day he stayed in his room. I could hear him talking on his cell phone to his friend, Steve. I thought, *he'll probably move in with Steve's parents until they discover that he isn't looking for a job.* Sunday was a quiet day. He got up and ate breakfast with me. He carried out the trash, without my asking him to do so. We acted civil to one another; I'm sure he had a lot on his mind.

Finally, Kent said, "I've been talking to Steve about joining the Marines. His dad was a Marine, and I think he wants Steve to go into the military. If we decide to do this, would you be okay with it?"

"I think you will develop good skills in the service and have the training to earn a living when you get out." I replied.

"We'll probably go down to the recruiting office tomorrow." He said.

I left for work on Monday morning, with hopes that Kent would follow through on joining the service.

When I got home that night Kent and Steve were at the apartment. They were all excited about the information they'd received while at the recruiting office. "We can join in the group that will be leaving next week, Mom. Are you sure that you're ok with this?"

"I think it's a great idea, for both of you." I replied.

The two of them retreated to Kent's room and made their plans on what to take with them. I think they had a list of property that would be allowed and things they needed to leave behind. I was excited that Kent had sought out the Marines. He'd take orders and learn from it. I was sure he was headed in the right direction.

After Steve and Kent left for basic training I was alone in my apartment. It was too quiet and it took some getting used to. I'd provided for my sons through good times and bad, but my job of raising them was over.

CHAPTER 15

Karen phoned me early one morning to tell me that Grandpa Fuller had passed away in the night. I was devastated. I called my boss to tell him that I needed to fly to Wisconsin for a few days. I needed to be there for Grandma Fuller and for Grandpa's funeral. They'd been such a big part of my life growing up and I hadn't been back to Holbrook in a lot of years. I had such an empty feeling and wished I'd kept in closer contact with them.

I made my flight arrangements then called my sister. "I'll need you to pick me up from the airport, Karen. We'll need to give all the support we can to Grandma Fuller. This is going to be tough on her. They had been married almost sixty years."

Karen said, "After the funeral is over and Grandma has had time to make some plans, she may decide to go into an assisted living home. Maybe she'll need our support in that decision."

We got through the funeral and I stayed overnight with Grandma. She seemed to be accepting the changes in her life. She kept thanking Karen and me for being there for her and Granddad. The idea of assisted living for her now that she was alone seemed to appeal to her. I hoped she'd follow through on it.

I flew back to Pasadena on Sunday.

Chapter 16

Over the next few weeks, I felt so lonely that I decided to take up a hobby to fill up my free hours. I signed myself up for a writing class at the local college. I'd always had my secretary compose any letters for me, but I felt that, as a professional woman with a good job, I needed to be able to write my own.

My first night in writing class I sat next to a terrific looking guy about my age. I liked his smile and the twinkle in his eyes. He introduced himself, "Hi, I'm Mark Dawson. And you are …?"

"I'm Jo Fuller and this is my first night in class," I replied.

"I thought I hadn't seen you here before. How advanced are you in the writing world?"

"I've worked for ten years with the Federal Government; however, when problems surface, my secretary has always been there to save my hide. I thought it was time for me to educate myself. My boss has told me that if I'd learn good writing techniques I could come into the office only a couple days a week for meetings and updates. It would be quite an advantage for me to work from home."

"Good thinking," Mark agreed.

We chatted until the instructor began speaking. I found out that first night in class that I fit somewhere in the middle of the group, as far as my writing knowledge was concerned. I felt comfortable, and the teacher was very good at explaining the terminology so we could understand it.

When the evening was over, Mark said, "Would you like to have a cup of coffee with me? It's only nine o'clock and the coffee shop is just around the corner."

"Sure", I said. "I don't have a lot of friends in the neighborhood."

At the coffee shop, we continued our conversation. I asked, "Have you lived in Pasadena long?"

"I'm a native, and have been here most all my life except for my years in the service. Maybe I can show you some of the landmark sights in this part of California sometime."

I didn't think he was pushy, just that he was a nice man. "I'd love that, Mark." I replied.

"I usually run in the park on Saturday and Sunday mornings, but, if you'll give me your phone number, I'll give you a call and we can plan something together."

"That sounds fun; thanks for asking. I'd better get going now. I'll see you next class."

I thought of Mark often. I thought that my life was so boring that he probably wouldn't want to date me. But I did need to start getting out more and enjoying life in the city. Maybe he would be the one to show me around town.

Mark called me two nights later. "I hope you don't think I'm too forward, but I've been thinking about you, and was wondering if you'd like to go up to San Francisco this week-end? They're having an old car show at the fairgrounds with classic cars from all over California."

"I've nothing planned and I'd love to go." I replied. I gave him my address.

"I'll pick you up at nine o'clock Sunday morning." Mark said.

When he arrived I was ready to go for the day. I had my water, some snacks, good walking shoes and my shades. "I'm really looking forward to this day, Mark."

"Let's rock and roll, "Mark said.

We found it easy to talk to one another on the ride to San Francisco. Mark had just separated from his wife. They'd been married for ten years with no children. She had been a nurse and Mark owned his own dog grooming business. I didn't pry into his life; he talked freely, and seemed okay with his decision to get a divorce. "My wife Sheila and I found that we just drifted apart. Perhaps if we'd had a family we'd have worked harder to stay together." he said.

"I don't know, Mark, if that would have made a difference or not. Raising kids is such a hard job. I did it for a lot of years by myself. When they fight you most of their lives, it becomes such a difficult task that you feel overpowered. Now that my sons, Eric and Kent, are out of the house, I look back and see a lot of my mistakes in trying to raise them. I played the hand that was dealt me but it wasn't easy being a single parent."

"I'm sorry you had it so rough, Jo." Mark said.

The day was so lovely and the scenery was beautiful. Just riding along with Mark was wonderful. I could tell he was a decent man, and I hoped he was enjoying himself with me.

The car show was interesting. Some of the cars were driven by owners who lived in the Bay area. Mark loved classic cars. We spent several hours moving from car to car, looking inside at all the restoration.

On the way back Mark said, "I'd like to take you to this little Italian restaurant I found in Pasadena. Are you up for some Italian food?"

"I love Italian food. I'm having so much fun today, Mark. Thanks for asking me to join you."

I wasn't looking for a permanent relationship; however, we did like being together. It was a lovely first date.

We continued to stop for coffee after class. Just having someone to laugh and talk with was a real treat for me. Mark had been operating his dog grooming business for years, and had handled all his own paper work without a secretary or help from his wife.

We were getting together on the week-ends to run in the park or go to the movies. Mark and I could laugh about anything. He liked to come by my apartment for a drink, even if it was just juice and nothing with alcohol.

"You're so much fun to be with, Jo." Mark said. "I've had a good time, every time we've been together."

"I feel the same," I replied. "I guess our meeting at the writing class was 'being at the right place at the right time.' "

On our third date, when we returned from the movies I asked Mark to come in and show me a better way to compose a certain letter. Mark solved the issue in no time. I threw my arms around his shoulders and hugged him. He stood up and kissed me. What a kiss it was for both of us. We stayed wrapped in an embrace and wanting more. We didn't fight the urges and headed for my bedroom. Mark was a wonderful patient man, and the sex was wonderful for both of us. He spent the night. We talked in the morning about our feelings for one another before heading out to our jobs. This relationship was building into something we both wanted and needed.

That night Mark phoned and said, "Could we get together this coming Sunday?"

He wanted to drive up the coast along the ocean, to Carmel. He picked some beautiful places to show me. He was telling me about receiving notice that the court date for his divorce was the coming Monday. He needed to talk, so I listened. "I've invested ten years with Sheila, but now it's time to move on." He talked about the two of us and how wonderful it was to have me in his life. I felt fortunate to have met Mark and knew he was a keeper. We were both adults, and at a point in our lives where we didn't want to waste time dating. We felt that we'd found one another, and needed to commit to each other.

The following Sunday Mark came over for brunch. He said the divorce was now final and he planned to move on with his life. "I know this is sudden, but you know how I feel about you, Jo, and I want us to get married as soon as we can make the arrangements. I think we both want the same thing."

"I'm ready to spend the rest of my life with you Mark; let's keep it simple, like going to the court house to tie the knot, then, a two day honeymoon down in San Diego."

"I'm going to pick up the marriage license tomorrow morning. We can get married on Friday morning if you can take the day off. I'll get my friend Matt to cover the store on Friday and Saturday."

"Oh, Mark, I'm so happy." I said.

I could hardly concentrate on my job the next few days. I told only my sister Karen, over the phone, of my plans to marry Mark.

Karen said, "I hope you two will be very happy. You deserve a good man and he sounds like a dream come true."

On Friday morning, May 27th, 1975, Mark picked me up at my apartment. I was wearing a new beige suit with a brown animal print blouse. I had on a pair of sling back heels in beige, and Mark commented, "Jo, you look like a beautiful model."

Mark had on a new brown suit with a light blue shirt and brown necktie. He looked so handsome. "You could model in that outfit, yourself." I replied.

We arrived at the courthouse on schedule. In just a short time I became Mrs. Mark Dawson. We left there and drove south to San Diego. Mark had made a reservation at the Sheraton Hotel. We checked in and changed our clothes to casual shorts, sandals, and tee shirts.

We grabbed a picnic basket from a little deli and made our way to a nearby park. Nothing fancy, but we just wanted to relax and enjoy being newlyweds. A bottle of good wine with cheese and sandwiches was the order of the day. "This is so enjoyable, Mark. I'm glad you suggested it."

We had two lovely days in the sun strolling around San Diego looking at the sights.

We returned to Pasadena Sunday night. Mark moved into my apartment on Monday after work. We settled down to cooking, watching movies together, and really getting to know one another.

Mark usually played darts with his buddies on Monday nights. I busied myself those nights with laundry, cleaning the apartment or just relaxing with a nice glass of wine in the tub.

We'd been married just two months, when disaster struck our world.

Mark's ex-wife, Sheila, called him at work to tell him that she was pregnant. They'd had one night of sex, before we met and married. She was certain the child was Mark's.

"I don't know what to do, Jo," Mark said. "Sheila said that she will get a blood test to determine if the baby is mine. I feel it could be but we tried for ten years and no children ever came along."

Sheila's pregnancy became the focus of our future together. I couldn't find words to describe my feelings on this latest turn of events. I knew Mark had always wanted to be a father, but this late in life a baby was a lot to consider. What about our life, our marriage: where did this leave us? Mark and Sheila were almost forty years old now. Shelia was adamant about the pregnancy and wouldn't consider an abortion.

Finally, the test results were given to Mark, in writing. He was the father of the child. I knew Mark was torn between going back to Sheila and trying again to have a family life with her and his baby and staying with me. He loved me and the new life we'd began, but our love was new and they had had ten years together.

I thought about the situation we were now in. I finally told Mark that I'd understand if he decided to go back to Sheila. I loved him enough to want him to experience being a father. He seemed saddened to lose me, but I assured him it was the right thing to do.

Mark moved out later that week and in with Shelia. I filed for divorce, and cried my eyes out. Over the next six weeks I suffered in silence alone in my apartment. I was devastated over our breakup and fell into a deep depression. I had a hard time dragging myself to work and back home at night. Mark wasn't a man you could forget easily. I thought I'd done the right thing by letting him go, but I was paying the price alone and with extreme regrets.

I talked to my sister at least once a week. She advised, "Stay busy, Sis. What happened wasn't any fault of yours."

I made myself get up and keep moving, trying to work through my disappointment over this huge loss.

Chapter 17

It's strange how some events happen in life; one door closes and another really does open. Within a month, my boss, Warren, came to me with a job change and promotion. It was a newly created traveling job that would move me into a leadership position. I would now have four people working under me in my department.

I needed this new direction in my career. I was excited and felt my years of hard work were finally being rewarded and recognized. I had always felt I did a good job but now obviously others did, too, and soon many more would be aware of it. There wasn't anything keeping me in Pasadena. I accepted the new job.

I did what any other professional would do with this kind of an opportunity; I went shopping! I needed some tailored business suits. I contacted a professional dresser and she was a big help in getting me dressed for this new position. I had tailored blouses made to go with my suits and found good comfortable walking shoes. I picked up a few accessories, and I was ready to travel. A good briefcase and a nice handbag finished off my professional look.

My first assignment was in Dallas, Texas. I packed my suitcase for warmer weather and off I flew.

Later I went on to Atlanta, Georgia and finally to Ft. Lauderdale, Florida.

Be careful what you wish for, as the old saying goes, I thought to myself. I'd always wanted a government job, and now I was in the receiving line and felt up to the task. *Bring it on!*

For the next eight years I traveled the United States and made several trips to London and Germany. I missed out on a lot of things while traveling, but it couldn't be avoided. The work I did was top secret and highly confidential.

On my first trip to London I had some free time in between meetings so I went to see several attractions in the West End. I also took in the financial district and saw the Tower of London. I did not go to any museums or operas but hoped to do so on another visit. I found myself relaxing and window shopping a lot while there.

Aunt Clara passed away while I was in England. Karen went to her funeral and gave our sympathies to Uncle Roy. Clara had been like a second mother to me, and will be in my heart forever.

Later that same month Grandma Fuller had a heart attack and died while in the assisted living home. Karen again paid our respects. I'll always have fond memories of my loving grandparents.

Kent called me every now and then and gave me updates on his training and what was going on in his life as a marine. He seemed to be adjusting well to military life. I was happy when he said he wanted to make a career of it.

I received no communication from my older son, Eric. I checked from time to time with military records but found no information. He did not communicate with Kent or any other family members. I feared the worst. Maybe he changed his mind about the army, and didn't sign up after all. Something had happened to him, but what? I had no answers.

CHAPTER 18

Years later, when I finally returned to Pasadena, I had a new work assignment. I'd lived out of my suitcase long enough. My traveling days were about over, and I was ready to settle down in one place. I found a new apartment, got my furniture out of storage and began life once again in sunny California.

My old car had quit running before I left town so I'd been using a rental car. I headed to a dealership to look for a replacement. A good looking salesman approached me. "Looking for new wheels?" he asked. "I'm Buzz Kennedy, and I'm at your service."

"I think I'd like to try a pickup truck. What about that black one?"

Buzz said, "That would be perfect for you. It has all the bells and whistles and gets very good gas mileage. Would you like to take it for a drive?"

"I would." I said. "Let's try it out."

"I'll get the key and be right back."

I got behind the wheel and we took off. We headed for the freeway and I liked the way the truck handled. "I think this's my vehicle," I said. "This is just what I've been wanting."

"That's what I like, a woman who knows what she wants and can make up her mind. Let's get back to the lot and get you signed up." Buzz said.

Buzz made small talk while the papers were being drawn up. He was an attractive guy with a beautiful tan and sparkling white teeth. He asked, "What do you do for a living, Jo?"

"I have a government job and just changed from a lot of traveling to a position here in town, and it sure seems good to be home again."

"Are you single, Jo?" Buzz asked.

I thought to myself, *he sure is a talker. He's in the right profession, selling cars.*

"Yes, I'm single and it's by choice."

Buzz said, "Well, I'll have to see what I can do to change your mind."

I laughed at his outspoken words. He was a huge flirt and I hadn't paid any attention to a man in so long I found him amusing.

As I got the paperwork completed and the keys in my hand, Buzz asked me for my phone number. Why I gave it to him I'll never know, but maybe I did it just to get out of there. I drove my new truck off the lot feeling good about my choice of transportation.

I called my good friend, Rita, and told her that I'd just bought a new pickup truck. I said, "I'll be right over to pick you up and we'll go for a ride." Rita was waiting outside when I pulled up to her apartment. She got in and I headed for the highway. We drove around Pasadena, talking and catching up on old times.

Rita said, "Oh, I almost forgot to tell you the latest on Mrs. Peterson who lives in my building. She has a little three pound Yorkie named Sandy and wants to find him a good home. She's going into an assisted living home, and can't keep him. You have often talked about getting a dog, but have been traveling too much. Now that you're back in town to stay, would you be interested in having him?"

"I would love it! How soon can we arrange it?"

"I think she's home right now. Let's stop over and see if she still has him."

We dropped in on Mrs. Peterson. She still had Sandy and after we visited awhile, she asked me to take her precious Yorkie and give him a good home. I promised her I would. We gathered up his food, his dish and his bed. I told her that I'd bring him by her place to visit once she got settled.

I thanked Rita for helping me get Sandy. I dropped her off at her place and headed back to my apartment. I was so happy to have company now, and Sandy was used to being held and cuddled. We were a perfect couple.

Not to my surprise, the phone call from Buzz came a couple nights later. He was a player and full of himself. I don't know why he zeroed in on me, but he wanted to know, "Will you go out with me on Saturday night?"

Against my better judgment I said "If we're going to the horse races, sure I'll go, Buzz."

When Buzz arrived for our date he had flowers for me. I thought, *how old fashioned is that?* He wanted to impress me, thus, the daisies. I invited him in and Sandy greeted him at the door. Buzz picked up the dog. I could tell he loved animals by the way he gently handled my three pound Yorkie. We had one thing in common - we both loved dogs.

"I got tickets to the football game; hope you like sports." Buzz said.

Now here was a man that I could relate to, "Forget the horse races, I love football. Let's go!" We had such a good time that night. We talked and laughed a lot. The home team won and we made plans to go again in two weeks, to the next home game.

Buzz told me on my doorstep, when he dropped me off, that he'd had a great time. He thought I was funny and a swell gal. I needed that kind of attention. It had been years since I'd been out on a date. He'd been around and dated a lot - I could tell. He was the kind of man who didn't like to be by himself. Women were treated well in Buzz's presence. I could use some attention by a man, and for now, Buzz was that man.

Of course I phoned my sister and told her about the date. She was glad that I was getting back into circulation. "You've been traveling the earth and haven't had much time to date. I'm glad you found Buzz. Enjoy your time together. I hope to get out there for a visit sometime this year. I miss you, Sis."

Over the next several months Buzz gave me the mad rush. He dropped all his old girlfriends and we dated exclusively. He had the gift of gab and was always talking. It made my ears ache at times, but I didn't say anything about it. His job at the car dealership was the kind of job where he needed to be aggressive, and talking was what he did best. He made a decent living selling cars and trucks.

The first night we spent together was a surprise for both of us. We weren't big drinkers, but he'd brought a bottle of wine over and I'd made dinner for us. We ate dinner by candlelight. The wine was delicious and before we knew it we were doing the touchy, feely thing. We both headed for the bedroom and would let happen, whatever happened. It was wonderful, the sex was terrific! It had been so long since I'd been intimate with anyone. When we woke up on Sunday morning he wanted to go at it again, which we did. He couldn't seem to get enough sex.

Finally, he jumped out of bed and headed for the shower. "We'd better hurry if we want to get to the game before kickoff." he said. I followed him into the shower as he was getting out.

"I'll make coffee while you get ready."

After we were dressed and had our coffee in carry out cups we headed to the football game. We had another great day. We had so much in common and could talk about any subject.

He dropped me off that night after we'd stopped for a light dinner.

"I'll call you" he said. We kissed a long kiss and he drove off.

On Monday at work, I thought about Buzz. I knew he'd been with a lot of women, but, there was something about him that I needed.

We continued to date and after a few months, he said one night, "You know Jo, we're a good match. You make me laugh and I adore you. Let's tie the knot, baby."

I was shocked! I said, "You came into my life quite by accident. It must have been a good omen for me to pick your dealership to look for a new truck. Life is short and we're not getting any younger, I'm ready to settle down to a life together with you."

"I'll let you do all the arrangements, Jo. You've been married a few times and know what to do." he said.

That was an understatement if ever there was one, I thought to myself. However, I did not take offense because it was true.

We married on November 17th, 1985. It was simple, with Rita as my attendant and Buzz's good friend from work, Zack, as his attendant. We had a terrific dinner at Fisherman's Wharf. Our friends returned to Pasadena and Buzz and I headed to Carmel for a couple of days.

Our honeymoon was second only to the one I'd experienced with Bud in the Bahamas years ago. We relaxed by the seashore and walked around Carmel. We window shopped the quaint little stores leading down to the beach. We were so happy to be together.

Once we returned, Buzz moved into my apartment because it was larger. He had a lot of clothes. I'd never seen a man who had such a large wardrobe. Plus, he had a lot of possessions he'd collected over the years. He must have saved everything from his childhood. We managed to get it all stored in the second bedroom closet.

Our days started off with my leaving the house to get to work at eight A.M. Buzz didn't need to be at work until ten. He worked some evenings until nine o'clock. That made our dinners very late. I'd never been one to have a big lunch and, therefore, I was always starving by seven. We discussed this problem and he suggested, "Why don't you go ahead and eat and just put a plate of food for me into the microwave. I can warm it when I get home."

I agreed to try it, and this seemed to work during the week for us. I did not really mind eating alone.

CHAPTER 19

We'd been married about six months, and I thought things were going well for us; but was I mistaken!

One morning, after I left for work, I realized I'd forgotten my brown shoes to go with the outfit that I was wearing that day. I was scheduled to give a presentation at 2 o'clock. I thought I could swing by the apartment and change shoes. When I opened the door to our apartment I could hear music and voices. I opened the bedroom door and was horrified to find Buzz and a redhead, in our bed!

"What the hell are you doing home?" he said.

"Better still, what the hell are you doing *making out* in our bed, while I'm at work?"

I said to the redhead, "Get dressed and get out of here. You can take this good for nothing son of a bitch with you!"

"You'd better have your things out of here by the time I get home tonight or I'll throw them out into the street!" I said to Buzz.

I grabbed my shoes, and left. I called Rita and asked her to go by and pick up Sandy. I didn't want Buzz to get any ideas about taking my dog. I told her briefly what had just happened at the apartment, and that I'd told him to leave.

"I'm so sorry, Jo. He didn't know how good he had it with you. Some men can't be true to one woman." She said.

Why hadn't I seen this coming? We had a lot of sex, anytime he wanted. I was a good cook; we liked to do the same things; what the hell was *wrong* with me that I couldn't keep a man?

Buzz was a big flirt with a lot of charm. I thought he'd leave all his womanizing behind once we were married. Now that I think back, he reminded me of my father. I'd been *played* by a player!

I stopped by Rita's on my way home from work to get Sandy. She said, "Buzz had two friends helping him move out when I stopped by to pick up Sandy."

"I'd better get home so the landlord can change the lock on my door tonight. See you, girlfriend, and thanks for looking out for my dog." I was so lucky to have Rita as a true friend.

I knew he wasn't worth it but I cried myself to sleep that night. No second chance for Buzz. *Do me once, shame on you, do me twice, shame on me*! I lived by that rule. This was the first time I'd picked a cheater for a husband. I was batting zero when it came to picking a *keeper.*

Our divorce became final on the day we would have been married one year. I tried to tell myself that things worked out for the best in the long run. Buzz would have cheated on me sooner or later and to have found it out early in the marriage was probably best.

CHAPTER 20

I now had a lot of time to think about my future. I wanted to get out of this damn town. Pasadena was full of bad memories that I wanted to forget. I asked my boss for a transfer.

I told Warren, "You can send me anywhere there's an opening. I need a change of scenery."

"Don't worry, Jo," Warren said. "I'll find something for you."

The offer came one month later. It was to the city of Tucson, Arizona. I'd always liked the desert and the hot weather. I started packing for the move.

When I arrived in Tucson the great multi-cultural influences were a constant fascination. From the mariachi musicians in the Mexican restaurants to the heavy Spanish influence in the architecture, I loved it all. I loved my new job and all of its responsibilities.

CHAPTER 21

One of the first people I met at work was Nellie Foster. She was the motherly type, and we hit it off right away. She jumped right in to make me feel welcome. I couldn't believe my good luck to find Nellie on my first day on the job. I gave myself to this friendship without reservation.

In a very short time, Nellie and I became very close confidants and good friends. She reminded me of Aunt Clara - always ready to help out in any way she could. I trusted her completely.

She said, "Jo, you should meet my son, Clayton. He'd be perfect for you."

Mildly curious, I asked "What does he do for a living?"

"He's an insurance agent here in Tucson. Why don't you join us for brunch on Sunday? You're so bubbly that I think you and Clayton would be a good match." I agreed to meet them for brunch at the local hotel that Sunday.

When Nellie introduced us, I could see the love in her eyes for her son. She adored him.

Clayton said, "Jo, you're one special gal according to my mother and she's usually right about most things."

I could see the way he treated Nellie, and that sold me on Clayton.

Clayton asked, "Jo, would you like to go to the horse races with me this coming Saturday night?"

How could he know that going to the races was one of my all-time favorite things to do? I went to Santa Anita as often as I could during the years I lived in Pasadena. I loved the ponies and thought to myself, *why not go*? "Sure, it sounds like fun to me," I said.

Clayton replied, "Why don't we go early and have dinner at the track before the races."

"Ok with me," I answered.

"I'll pick you up at six."

He seemed to be a take charge fellow. He was about six foot tall and had broad shoulders. I liked his square chin and dark eyes. He was the first man I'd dated since my divorce. I wasn't looking for another permanent relationship, just trying to make some new friends in Tucson. After brunch we parted and I didn't hear from him again until he knocked on my door Saturday night at six.

"Wow," he said, "You look terrific in that suit and hat. Red is your color."

How nice to be complimented. Those words meant more than a look in the mirror to tell me how I looked. Clayton, too, looked terrific. The idea of pairing hip-hugging jeans with a nice sports jacket was a new dress code that I found particularly charming in the southwest.

We didn't have that comfortable feeling you get with someone when you have known them over time and have shared experiences. Our only shared area was *his mom*. Conversation was a little awkward at first as we talked about the weather and then a little about our work.

"Do you like pets?" I asked him on the ride to the track. I was making small talk so we could get to know one another better.

"I do, but never had any. I just didn't want to be tied down with the responsibility of caring for an animal. Do you have a pet?"

"Yes, I do; his name is Sandy. He's a Yorkie and I've had him for seven years. I had to leave him with my girlfriend, Rita, back in Pasadena, until I found an apartment that accepts animals. She'll put him on an airplane next Saturday and I can pick him up at the airport. I can hardly wait for him to arrive. I miss him so much." Clayton had no reply.

When we reached the racetrack we made our way to our reserved table in the dining area. The waiter brought the menus and we began to look them over.

"I hope they have seafood, it's one of my favorites."

"Ugh, I hate seafood of any kind," Clayton replied

"You're probably a meat and potatoes man."

"No. That just clogs up your arteries."

We weren't agreeing on any food selections that night. When the waiter arrived to take our orders, I said, "I'll have the shrimp with a salad. Could I have the dressing on the side please?" Clayton took awhile to order then made his choice.

He said, "I'll have the pasta plain, no sauce and a salad with no dressing."

Strange food selection, I thought, but to each his own. We ate in silence. I found it hard to talk to Clayton at times, but figured it was because we knew so little about one another. So far no little red flags were waving danger signs. I was so excited about being at the track that I doubt if anything could have put a major damper on my enthusiasm. I was out for a night of fun and that was damn well what I was going to have.

Clayton said, "Let's go down to the paddock and take a look at the horses."

"I'm ready."

The horses were walking around in the paddock. When I saw the number four horse, lifting his head high and strutting around while being lead by his trainer, I said, "That's my pick, the number four horse. Which one do you like?"

"I haven't picked one yet. I don't see any that I'd put my money down on," he said.

We hurried back to our table after I placed my bet. Just as we got seated, the first race went off. My number four horse was coming up nicely on the back stretch doing well and as it rounded the final curve for the finish line I said, "Come on baby!" I was jumping up and down with excitement as I held on to Clayton's arm. My horse won the race. "I won, I won," I shouted out to the whole dining area. I'd bet fifteen dollars and had won fifty bucks! I was so excited. Clayton just looked at me like I was a crazy person.

"What's wrong?" I said, as I sat down. I knew he was probably embarrassed by my actions but I'm an excitable person and winning a horse race was something to stand up and shout about as far as I was concerned. It seemed strange to me that Clayton didn't place a bet all night. Why would a person go to the races and not bet on the horses? I thought to myself *what is it going to take to get him to relax and enjoy the evening?*

Clayton said, "I've never been to the track before tonight. I knew you liked the horses because you'd told my mother about your good times at the racetrack. I'm glad we came and that we had fun tonight."

He'd taken me to a place that his mother suggested. Didn't he have any self confidence in making a choice of his own? I began to wonder about Clayton. He was definitely different from any guy I'd ever dated.

I continued to bet the rest of the races, winning a little and losing at times. It was fun for me like back at the track in Santa Anita. I could tell, however, that Clayton really wasn't into horseracing. I felt he had probably only suggested our evening there because he knew I'd like it.

On our way home, Clayton said, "Would you like to go water skiing tomorrow? My friend, Richard, from work has a ski boat, and he and his wife, Rene, want me to bring you along for an afternoon on the lake.

I didn't want to hurt his feelings, so I said, "I'm not good at skiing, but I do love being out on the water and catching some rays. I'd love to meet them."

When Clayton pulled up on Sunday morning, I had my bathing suit on under my shorts and tee shirt. I grabbed my bag with water, sun tan lotion, sun glasses, and snacks. "I'm ready to hit the water," I said.

When we arrived at the dock, Clayton introduced me to Richard and Rene. They were a quiet couple so I tried to keep the conversation going. "What do you do for a living?" I asked Rene.

"I work from home on the computer. Richard sells insurance at the agency where Clayton works."

Silence followed and I thought to myself, *this will be a strange afternoon if I have to do all the talking. Clayton had better join in soon.* I wasn't used to making a lot of small talk with people that I'd just met. Finally I heard Richard and Clayton talking about work. I took the opportunity to remove my tee shirt and shorts and lie back on my towel. I got out my sun tan lotion and put it on. I was ready to catch some sun. I guess I'd drifted off to sleep, because I awoke to hear Richard talking.

We were out on the lake now and he was saying, "Who wants to go up first?"

Clayton didn't say a word. I'd already told Clayton that I didn't water ski, and that I was along today just for the sun and relaxation. Richard was waiting for someone to speak up.

I said, "Why not let Rene go first? I'm not into skiing. I'll just watch."

Rene jumped into the water and Richard operated the boat. She was a good skier and got up on her first try. All that afternoon she was the only one who skied.

On the way home I asked Clayton why he wanted to go water skiing if he wasn't going to try to get up on skis. His answer to my question was that he just wanted to be with me, and thought I'd enjoy the afternoon out on the lake.

I could tell Clayton was getting ideas about the two of us committing to each other. He was the only fellow I'd dated since moving to Tucson. I had been asked out to lunch at work by a co-worker Dan Willis but had to take a rain check that day because I needed to finish some paperwork on my lunch hour. He didn't ask me again so I supposed he'd moved on to someone else.

I said to Clayton "Let's take this relationship slowly. I'm not ready to rush into another marriage." Clayton had some quirks that seemed strange to me. I needed to know more about him. We hadn't dated long, and I wasn't feeling that comfortable around him, but he wanted more of my time.

On Saturday we went together to the airport to pick up my precious dog, Sandy. When I finally got my little baby in my arms I was so glad. His little tail wagged and he was happy to lick my face and be held, curled up in my arms. Sandy paid no attention to Clayton.

"You'll learn to love him, he's a sweetie," I said, but Clayton had no comment.

I found out at work that the company was sending me to London to do a presentation on the manuals that I had written for the latest project. When I mentioned it to Clayton, he said, "Why don't you see if they can send someone else?"

"Are you kidding me? I've worked for the past fifteen years for the Federal Government, and this project is one that I'm very proud of. I'll be leaving in about a week or two."

My birthday was coming up on March 22nd. Clayton wanted to throw me a 50th birthday party. I thought that was nice of him and told him just make it a few close friends. When I walked into the Holiday Inn banquet room that night there were a lot of balloons and flowers throughout the room. A buffet line was set up, and the food was excellent. After we'd eaten Clayton grabbed a fork and began to clang a water glass to get everybody's attention.

"I have an announcement to make. As you know tonight is this wonderful gal's birthday, and I want to surprise her by asking for her hand in marriage!"

I was so shocked! I could only utter, "You sure know how to surprise a gal."

Clayton said, "I'll take that as a yes," as he grabbed me and kissed me.

I was speechless. I didn't want to spoil a party given for me, but I hadn't even entertained the thought of us getting married. But if Clayton loved me this much, surely I would learn to love him back.

On the car ride home, Clayton said, "I'll take care of getting an appointment with the judge on Friday, if you can take a half day off."

I knew I should discuss my true feelings with him, but he seemed to be so in charge, so I went along with the plan. What poor timing for a wedding. We hardly knew one another and I was leaving for London soon.

Chapter 22

We arrived at the court house on Friday afternoon, and within half an hour I became Mrs. Clayton Foster.

Our first night as newlyweds was a huge disappointment for me. As we were getting undressed for bed, Clayton said "I'm exhausted tonight, could we just cuddle, if you don't mind?"

What could I say? This wasn't anything I'd ever experienced before.

In the morning over breakfast, I said, "You know I leave for London this Sunday and I'll be gone for a week."

Clayton looked at me and didn't say a word.

"Can you drop me at the airport?" I asked.

"I suppose you want me to look after your dog too," he said.

"That would be nice of you," I replied. "Love me, love my dog," I laughed.

I left on my trip and didn't hear a word from my new husband all week. I phoned him and left a message for him to pick me up at the airport on Saturday. When I arrived back in town he wasn't anywhere in sight, so I caught a taxi and came home to the apartment. I opened the door and found Clayton lying on the couch watching TV.

"Too much trouble to come pick me up?" I asked, with anger in my voice.

"I didn't realize the time. It just got away from me." He replied.

I picked up my little Sandy and realized immediately that something was wrong. His eyes were glazed over. "I'm taking this dog to the vet." I grabbed my purse, car keys, and the dog, and ran for the car. When the vet checked Sandy over, he could tell the dog was sick. "I'll take some blood and send it off to the lab. Meanwhile why don't you leave Sandy here so I can observe him over the weekend? You can pick him up on Monday after work."

When I arrived back at the apartment Clayton said, "You care more about that damned dog than you do me!"

"Clayton, how can you say such a thing? You knew I had a dog when you started dating me. You also knew when you married me that I'd have to travel, due to my job with the government. Let's not fight and argue tonight. I just got home."

He whined, "You should tell them that you are a newlywed and now have a husband at home."

I thought to myself that they'd be real happy to hear that one from a grown responsible woman concerning her position at work. Clayton was being unreasonable on this issue.

He was beginning to get on my last nerve over some of the simplest things. Why I didn't take more time before jumping into this marriage, I'll never understand. The traveling that I had to do was probably the only way we were staying married, if the truth were known. I couldn't imagine putting up with his whining on a daily basis.

"I'm hungry," Clayton said. "Let's go eat."

"I'll change my shoes and be ready to go in a few minutes."

When we were seated at the restaurant, we ordered our food and ate in silence. I said, "After I get the laundry caught up tomorrow, I'm yours for the day. Have you thought of anything you'd like to do, dear?" I tried to smooth things over after the last angry words from him regarding my dog and my traveling.

"I'll go to the market while you do laundry, and we can plan something that we'll both enjoy, for the afternoon and evening," he said.

I thought to myself now that we were off the unpleasant subjects of dog and travel we could have a pleasant evening together.

We spent the evening watching a movie on TV. On Sunday, we had breakfast and went for a leisurely walk around the lake on our apartment grounds. Clayton seemed content with no more outbursts. I took a short nap and made dinner. It was a quiet time for me to recover from my jet lag and the trip to London.

On Monday morning, I arrived at my office early and was checking my papers from my trip. I was just going into a briefing regarding the presentation I'd given in London when the phone rang.

"Hi Jo," said the vet. "You're going to be upset, and I hate to have to tell you this, but Sandy died in the night. He may have eaten some spoiled food. The blood work will tell us more, so I will call you when the tests come back. I know he was special to you and I'm very sorry."

I fought back the tears. I couldn't fall apart at this time. The de-briefing was to start in ten minutes. I'd have to suck it up and grieve for Sandy later, in private. Somehow, I got through the morning's meeting. I asked Warren if I could leave early. I told him about the death of my dog and he told me to go on home.

"You have a lot of comp time built up, Jo. Take a day or two off if you need to."

"Thanks Warren. I appreciate your understanding about my loss."

When I got home I told Clayton that Sandy had died. He held me close for a few minutes.

"You'll get over it," he said.

How cold and indifferent he seemed. My deep feelings over the loss of Sandy didn't seem to reach him. I had loved my sweet little dog and I grieved for him in silence.

Over dinner that night, I hated to tell Clayton the news I'd found out at work that day.

"I know you're not going to like hearing this news, but at today's briefing, my boss informed me that he wants me to fly to Germany and give the same presentation again next week."

Clayton sat there silent for a few minutes before he said, "You know something, Jo? I married you to have a partner. I thought you wanted that, too, but it seems our lives aren't going to allow us much time to spend together."

I knew I'd have to choose my words carefully. "Clayton, all my life I've worked to get the position I currently hold. I've found a lot of satisfaction in achieving the goals that I've set for myself. You aren't asking me to give all that up now, are you?"

Clayton sighed. "I know your job means more to you than I do. I'm far down on the list of your needs and wants. Or so it seems to me." I didn't have an answer for that statement.

He grabbed his jacket and headed out the door. I thought to myself, that he needed some time to re-think my position and his feelings regarding our marriage. We'd married too soon without really knowing one another. He resented the time I spent on my job away from him and yet traveling from time to time was a big part of my work with the Federal Government. Somewhere in this relationship we would have to reach a solution. Clayton either wanted me and the marriage badly enough to find contentment as things were or he'd have to decide to fold up and move on alone. I had a feeling he did not want to be alone but rather wanted me to give in and do things his way. He wanted to *own* me and tell me what to do and that was his first big mistake. He certainly didn't know that I was a take charge kind of woman and had been paddling my own canoe for a lot of years and could do so very nicely without any help from a man.

We got through the week with one night of love making. He was not a good lover, and I began to question *why, oh why, did I now find myself in this position?* I knew why; and I had to admit I'd jumped in before I knew Clayton's moody disposition. I didn't think it was anything I could fix for us. I had my doubts that we could survive this marriage - or whether I even wanted to.

CHAPTER 23

In no time at all I was in the air again, on my way to Germany. Stanley Bailey, my co-worker, was going along on this trip. He also had to give a presentation on his end of the project. I'd met Stan and his wife Virginia at a company picnic that last summer. They were a very nice, happily married couple. I had not mentioned to Clayton that Stanley would be going as he seemed to be jealous over a lot of things.

In Germany we only had time for our presentation. No tours or shopping this time like I had enjoyed my last trip to Munich. I saw that there were Hop Off buses and trolley tours. If you get to an attraction and aren't interested in spending a lot of time there you can just hop back on the bus and continue on to places that appeal to you. This trip, however, was fully scheduled, with no time for relaxing or night life.

When I arrived home at the airport, Clayton was there to pick me up. He kissed me, and acted like he had really missed me. "Let's go to dinner and talk," he said. "I think we have a few issues that need to be addressed."

I was glad he wanted to talk because I knew I couldn't go on with this marriage the way it was. I really felt we'd married too soon and didn't know each other or what we expected from one another. If Clayton needed me to be joined at the hip with him we definitely would be headed for the divorce courts. I also wasn't happy with him in the lovemaking department. Clayton did not know how to satisfy a woman. That would be a touchy subject to deal with if we ended up in marriage counseling. Most men do not appreciate being told they are sorry in the bedroom. Really, though, at this point I wasn't interested in trying to salvage the marriage. It isn't in my nature to give a guy more chances when I've decided that he's history as far as my life with him is concerned. I was willing to admit the marriage was a huge mistake and move on.

We had finished our dinner when in walked Stan with his wife, Virginia. They stopped by our table. I stood up, and introduced them to Clayton. I hugged Stan, and then Virginia. Clayton didn't even offer his hand to Stan. We chatted for a couple minutes and then their table was ready. As they were leaving our table Stan said, "I suppose you haven't had time to tell Clayton about Germany yet."

I could just see the smoke coming out of Clayton's ears. Stan and his big mouth! What poor timing!

"Come on, we're leaving." Clayton screamed.

I did not want to make a scene in the restaurant, so after he paid the bill we walked out to the parking lot. The valet brought my car around.

"Get in." he ordered me into the car.

I thought to myself, *this will be quite a ride home!* Little did I know what he had on his mind. His face was beet red and his jawbone was set like he was full of anger. He headed in the opposite direction of our apartment.

I asked, "Where are we going?"

Clayton shouted, "Just *shut* your mouth! I know that you've been sleeping around on me and now I know with whom. Stan! I could see the way he looked at you tonight, you bitch! You are a good for nothing *whore*!"

"What are you talking about?"

"I'll show you just what I think of you," he said as he drove out of town and into the desert.

"I want out of this car!" I screamed.

"I don't give a *damn* what you want," he swore.

Finally, he stopped the car in the middle of nowhere. It was pitch dark that night. He shut off the lights, got out of the car, and came around to my side. He opened the door and proceeded to drag me out of the car by my hair.

"Stop this *nonsense*!" I begged him.

He pushed me so hard from behind that I lost my balance and fell onto my hands and knees in the gravel. I could feel my hands bleeding and I knew my knees were cut too. One of my shoes came off and he threw it far out into the desert.

"Clayton, you're out of control."

He continued to rant and rave calling me foul names. I feared for my life. My cell phone rang and I *pleaded* for him to let me answer it. "It could be your mother trying to reach me about my trip." When I said *your mother* something clicked in his mind and he cooled down.

"Get back in the car." he said quite calmly.

I did as I was told.

We drove home without another word. I was weeping quietly. I did not want to anger Clayton further.

When we arrived in our parking space, he mumbled, "I think I'd better stay at the lodge tonight."

I sobbed, "I think that would be best."

He handed me my keys, then got into his car and drove off.

Breaking down into gasping sobs, I ran quickly into our apartment. I was so glad to be home, safe and alive! My cell phone rang as I was washing the gravel off my hands and knees. I picked up the phone, and heard Clayton barking at me.

"You *bitch!* I suppose you're calling the police on me right now! That ride out in the desert was just what you deserved and if I get the chance to do it again, you *won't make it back*!

"And what's more, just so you know this: your little dog ate that poisoned meat I fed him, like *the stupid mutt* he was."

I slammed my cell phone shut. He'd *killed* my precious pet! What kind of a *monster* had I married?

I picked up my phone and called the police. "I want to make a complaint against my husband, please come immediately!"

The officers arrived a few minutes later, and took pictures of my knees and hands. I explained the terrible ordeal that I had suffered, and Clayton was picked up later that night from the Lodge. He was sent to the local hospital for observation and was eventually committed to a mental institution. The authorities informed me that Clayton had had a nervous breakdown the year before we met. He'd been in the institution for five months that time. I arranged for a restraining order for him to stay away from me indefinitely.

I left a note on Nellie's desk at work on Monday, asking her to meet me at the coffee shop in the building after work.

She arrived and we hugged. I said, "Nellie, it isn't easy for me to cut all ties with you. I thought of you as the mother I lost years ago. But Clayton is a very sick man, and you misled me by not telling me of his past history and his breakdown last year. Do you realize the danger you put me in? He even *poisoned* my little dog, Sandy."

Nellie apologized, saying, "Jo, I'm so sorry you had to go through all that with Clayton. I feel responsible in a lot of ways. I was so sure he had recovered and was back to his old self. Believe me, I never meant you any harm."

"I'm moving on with my life and I won't be seeing you or Clayton again," I told her. "I want nothing to do with either of you from now on." I picked up my purse and briefcase and left the coffee shop.

I divorced Clayton soon after this meeting.

CHAPTER 24

Now, after reading my story, I suppose you can see my mistakes in this final choice of a husband. I had once again moved too fast and too soon. If I'd taken more time and listened to my gut instincts, I wouldn't have put myself through all this grief. I might have been able to see by Clayton's strange ways that he was mentally unbalanced. I know now, and have made my decision to quit looking for *Mister Right*. I'm grateful to still be among the living.

This last marriage and divorce had left me feeling empty. *I'd tried to love them all.* I realized that making quick decisions to marry men that I hardly knew had caused me so much sorrow. That last night with Clayton, I was lucky to get out with my *life.* He could have killed me out there in the desert. I shudder to even think about it.

CHAPTER 25

My thoughts drifted to my sister Karen back in Wisconsin. We both must have been feeling our separation, because she called me that very day and said, "Sis, I miss you. I've sold my house here in Holbrook, and I'd like to move to Tucson to be closer to you. Do you think you can help me find a house?"

I was ecstatic! "Of course I can," I replied. "I found mine and just love living in a house rather than an apartment. I'd love for us to live close again. How soon can you get here?"

"Well, I'll close on the house on the tenth of October. If you'll give me the name of a storage company I'll have my things shipped out to Tucson. I sold my car to my daughter, so can you pick me up at the airport?"

"You can count on it, and you'll stay with me while we look for your new home. Just a minute, I'll get the phone book and give you the number. I'll take a few days off from work when you get here and we'll house-hunt. This is the best news I've had in months. I'll see you soon."

I picked Karen up at the airport. We hugged and it felt so good to reconnect with my sister. "I can't believe this is happening, I never thought you and Junior would be divorced after thirty some years. I thought you were happy."

"Well, Junior got that forty year itch, as some men do, and he found himself a younger woman. I'd spent so much time keeping a house, and looking after the family, I didn't see it coming. I guess he wanted a little spice in his life. You know how they think the grass is always greener on the other side of the fence? Well, that's what happened to Junior. Sissy is very upset with her Dad over our divorce. Brad doesn't say much about it. He thinks it's our business, and stays out of it. I don't mind being on my own; really I don't. I've spent a lot of years giving and putting others first, and now it's my time to enjoy my choices. I'll get back into dating and maybe find me a man who will want me for me. With fifty years of experience I should appeal to somebody. I'm in no hurry, and for now I'm enjoying being single and on my own. The kids will adjust to the divorce in time."

"Well, Karen, you'll have to look for that man on your own. I've been down that road too many times and it didn't work out for me. I've had my heart broken into a million pieces and cried a river of tears over my disappointments caused by bad choices of men. Some of them were worth it but most of them were not. I plan to go it on my own from here on out."

"I understand your feelings on that subject, Sis." Karen said.

Karen found a house in a couple of weeks. It was a little two bedroom yellow bungalow with white shutters and a whitewashed fence. We got all her belongings from the rented storage unit. I helped her put away her dishes, and soon she was settled in. She made the adjustment to Arizona and had no trouble finding her way around Tucson. Some women, after a divorce, have a hard time making decisions but Karen was up for making choices on her own; in fact she was like a kid again and enjoying every moment of it.

"Let's make Saturday mornings our coffee catch up time, ok?" I suggested one day. "I'm retiring from my job at the end of the year and I'll have a lot of free time then."

"You got me, sister; I'm yours on Saturdays from now on. I think it's a great idea and it'll give us a chance to catch up on a lot of years of separation," Karen replied. She added, "I want to get a dog soon."

"I miss my little Yorkie, too. You and I can go pet shopping together." I said.

Karen agreed, and then added, "Oh, by the way, I always forget to ask, what are my nephews doing these days?

"Kent is retired from the service and working with Tidwell's Computer Company in Phoenix. He's got a girlfriend, Marianne, who works for the airlines. We can drive up some Saturday and surprise him. I don't know if I'll ever find out what happened to Eric. I try not to dwell on it." I said.

During our coffee chats on Saturdays, we talked and talked about our childhoods. We found that although we are different individuals, with a variety of life's experiences, we have similar feelings because of the same alcoholic parents. It's unfair that events happened as they did. That unconditional love you should expect to experience as a child just wasn't there for us.

We talked about our memories of the past. We agreed that we had lacked nurturing, and both of us had suffered depression over the years, stemming from unresolved and delayed grief over Mom's death.

One Saturday I said, "It took me almost fifty years, but I finally forgave Mom. She was in so much pain dealing with Dad that she felt suicide was her only way out."

Karen nodded. "I'd probably have been dead too, years ago, if it hadn't been for you looking out for me, Sis. I'll love you forever for being my protector throughout my childhood. Who knows how I might have turned out if you hadn't stepped in to guide me during my rebellious years? Our childhood was stolen from us and we never developed a strong sense of self worth. I'm now regaining my independence and I like it very much. I see how well you've succeeded in your professional career even when your personal life was in the toilet. Let's not lose what we've found now that I'm living here."

CHAPTER 26

Little did we know what joy the next event that happened in our lives would bring us. When the phone rang at my house on Saturday morning, I yelled to Karen, "Can you get the phone? It's in the bedroom on the charger."

"Sure thing," she replied.

I poured coffee into two mugs, then cut some cinnamon rolls and put them on the table. I heard Karen say "Hello," but she then continued to listen and I was wondering who it could be since she didn't know that many people here in Tucson. Soon she appeared in the doorway and handed me the phone.

"It's Kent and he has wonderful news. I think you'd better sit down."

I sat on a kitchen chair and reached for the phone. "Hi Son," I said. "What's up? Did you run off and get married?"

"No, Ma, nothing like that. Are you sitting down? I heard from Eric last night." I was shocked! I could hardly catch my breath.

"He's alive! Oh Kent, your brother has come back to us after all the years of not knowing what happened and fearing the worst. Where is he now? How soon can he get here?"

"Mom, slow down and let me talk. I'll fill you in on what I know," Kent continued. "He found me through my military records and found out that I was living in Phoenix. I'm listed in the phone book so he called information and got my number. He's living in Chicago, currently at home on crutches with a broken ankle. He wants to get together with all of us as soon as possible and will fly down this coming week-end. He has quite a story and wants to tell us in person."

"Do you have his phone number? Can I call him right now?"

"I do and here it is. I'll sign off now and hopefully see you two this week-end."

"Goodbye for now. Thanks for the wonderful news. You've made an old woman so happy! I can't begin to tell you how much. Tell Marianne hello for me. Love you, Son."

As soon as he hung up, I handed the phone to Karen. "Here, you had better dial it. I'm too anxious."

Karen dialed Eric's number and soon they were talking back and forth. She handed me the phone and said "Eric wants to talk to you, Sis."

"Hello, Son. I never thought this day would come. I feared the worst when we didn't hear from you over the years."

"I know, Mom, and I want to tell you what happened and all about my life; but I want to be there in person to do it. I'll get a flight out of here early Friday morning and Kent can pick me up in Phoenix later that afternoon. We'll drive down to Tucson and can all spend the weekend together."

"That sounds great. Karen and I will be waiting for the two of you." I closed my phone and began to weep. As the tears flowed, Karen and I hugged and cried together.

Karen said "I'm so happy for you and Kent, Sis. I know what you've been through not knowing if Eric was still alive. Now you will be able to reconnect and pick up the pieces where you left off." She paused. "Yes, there is a God."

On Friday after work I picked up some groceries so we would have plenty of food in the house for the weekend. Karen planned to come over about seven that evening and we would wait for the boys to arrive from Phoenix. I was so excited I couldn't sit still. I kept pacing the floor back and forth. Finally Karen arrived and she was just as nervous as I.

Karen said "I called my kids and told them their cousin Eric was alive and coming tonight along with Kent from Phoenix. They are very happy and relieved for all of us. Sissy says we need to plan a family reunion in the future so the cousins can get reconnected to the family."

We heard a car pull into the driveway. "I bet that's the boys." I ran out the door and flew to the car with Karen right beside me.

Kent turned off the engine and came around to open Eric's door and help him stand upright. We were all trying to hug one another and Eric was trying to balance himself and get the crutches under his arms. We were laughing and so excited to see each other. Eric looked so good. He still had a lot of curly hair like Mom's and Kent's. There was no mistaking Eric - he looked a lot like Grandpa Fuller from pictures of Grandpa's younger years. I took him into my arms and did not want to let go. I could have crumbled into a heap right there in the driveway with relief, but I wanted to stay strong for my sons. We finally all got inside and seated comfortably in the living room.

Eric said "Mom you look terrific! You've kept slim and you still have a full head of black hair. You do too, Aunt Karen. How do you gals stay so young looking? I'm shocked that neither of you are currently married. What's up with that, Mom?"

"Just listen to him, Karen," I laughed. "Well, we've both had a lot of years of married life, Son. Let's just leave it at that."

"Where do you think he got that gift of gab? Does he sound like our old man or what?" I continued, feeling so contented.

I looked back at my sons. "What do you boys want to drink? I have coffee, beer, sodas, and iced tea."

"I'll take a beer now that I'm not driving anymore tonight." Kent said.

"Make it iced tea for me" Eric said.

Karen and I were drinking iced tea already so she said, "Let me get it, Sis, you just sit there and relax."

Eric looked from me to Kent. "I hope I'm not going to bore all of you with the story of my life after seventeen, but I wanted to be here to explain why I didn't stay in touch over the years."

Karen returned with their drinks. "Your mom has food if you two want to eat, either now or later." She sat down to listen to Eric.

"We ate on the drive down, but thanks anyway." Kent said.

"First tell us how you got the broken ankle." Karen said.

"I stepped backward while loading some equipment into one of one of our trucks. Just a misstep on uneven ground and down I went. It's healing well and I'll soon be able to throw away the crutches."

Then Eric began to tell us what happened after he got on the bus at the age of seventeen with the other recruits heading to San Diego from Pasadena. "We made a stop for sodas and a bathroom break. I was having some doubts about what I was doing joining the army. I was sitting in the seat with a Mexican fellow - Remy Garcia – that I knew slightly from home. He was saying that he too was having second thoughts about what he was about to do. We began to talk and decided the military life wasn't for us. We planned to get off and not get back on when the bus stopped the next time. And that's what we did. Instead of going inside the rest area, we ran around to the back of the bathrooms and out into the desert."

"When we saw the bus pull away we realized that we were miles from anywhere," Eric continued. "The sun was scorching hot and we had no hats to cover our heads. Nothing to do but walk down the road and hope someone would give us a ride some of the way to San Diego. We certainly were not thinking clearly on that one, but in less than an hour of walking, a farm truck came along and the farmer picked us up and took us all the way to San Diego. What a break for us. We were a little sun burnt and thirsty but otherwise ok.

"When we looked around Remy said he'd been in San Diego before and had crossed the border into Mexico from there. He was twenty years old and had carried drugs across the border a time or two for his uncles who lived in Mexico. When he was younger the authorities didn't check so closely and he had stashed drugs in his shoes and the lining of his hat.

"Since we had no way to make money he said we should go to his Uncle Roberto's place. We crossed the border into Tijuana. Of course the uncle was looking for a couple of green horns like us to transport drugs across the border. On our first attempt at it we got caught. The Mexican authorities threw us into a smelly jail and it was horrible! They left us there for hours without food or water. We had one little blanket each and a small pillow. We tried to sleep but of course we couldn't. It was such an awful situation! Nothing like I'd ever experienced before, and I thought my life was doomed. Finally, the next morning the guard came and got us and we went before a judge or magistrate. He read the charges and asked 'Do you have anything to say before I announce your fate?'

"Of course we were scared and afraid to speak and when nothing came out of our mouths, the magistrate said, 'I will give you two years in our jail and hope you think long and hard if you ever want to transport drugs again.'

"We were escorted back to jail and to our separate cells. They brought us food and water. Remy called out to me and said 'I'm sorry I got you into this mess, Eric.'

"I said to him 'No one forced me into it, so I'll just do my time.' I felt like a piece of shit, lower than a thief. I did not want to call you with that kind of news, Mom.

I'd gotten myself into this situation and I should have known better. You had raised me not to go against the law and now I'd have to pay the price.

"During my two years in jail I learned a lot of Spanish. I had to in order to know what was going on in that hell hole. It became my second language. I grew up in a hurry and realized I'd be stronger from the experience." He added earnestly, "I promised myself that I would never do anything underhanded again."

CHAPTER 27

E ric's saga continued. "On the day we were released from jail, Remy and I had fifteen dollars between us. It was a hot sticky afternoon and we headed for the first watering hole we could find. The bar was in full swing and crowded. We ordered two Coronas and sat down at a table.

"A film crew was in the bar and the foreman got up on a chair and whistled for attention. The bar grew quiet and he proceeded to say, 'We're looking for someone who speaks English and Spanish well, to work on stringing lights and laying cables for our company. We make movies all over the world and you'd have to travel most of the time.'

" 'I'm your man,' " I said, with my hand in the air.

"He said, 'what's your name, son?' "

"I'm Eric Robinson from Pasadena, California, sir."

" 'How old are you?' he asked."

"I'll be twenty next month."

"He said, 'Come up to the bar, son, and we'll talk.' "

"I looked at Remy. I hated to leave him but he had family there in town and I needed to look out for myself. I made my way up to the bar and the foreman introduced himself.

" 'My name is Cliff Edgar, and this fellow here is my right hand man, Frog. Well, not really; it's Fred Woodward but we call him Frog. We need a strong fellow like yourself to help us; we pay good money if you're willing to travel on the job. Are you married?' "

"I replied, 'No, and don't plan to be.' "

" 'That's good because we're in some towns for only six weeks or so then on to another gig. We can keep you employed, Eric, and this is a good job for a single fellow.' "

"I'm your man. When do I start?"

" 'We're finished on this job and packing up our gear tomorrow. Why don't you come with us when we leave the bar and we'll fill out your work papers. You can bunk in with the crew tonight; that way you'll be ready to help load up tomorrow morning.' "

" 'I'll just say good bye to my buddy Remy and be with you in a couple of minutes.' I walked over and extended my hand to Remy."

"He had a grin on his face as he stood up and grabbed my hand and shook it. He said, 'Good luck, friend. I'm happy for you. Put this past two years behind you and get on with your life, hombre.' "

Eric paused. "I hope this story isn't boring all of you. I tend to stretch it out, but there's a lot to tell."

"Son, we could never be bored listening to you and learning what you've been through. Does anybody need another drink before Eric continues?"

Kent said, "I can drink another beer, but first I'll need to use the bathroom."

Eric added, "I'll have another iced tea and bring on the snacks. I'll get my crutches and make my way to the bathroom, too, before I start talking again."

Karen and I headed for the kitchen and prepared some chips and dip. I'd cut up some apples earlier so I arranged them on four plates and drizzled the slices with caramel sauce. We got their drinks and ours refilled and got back to the living room. We were seated when the boys returned, and Eric was ready to continue with his story.

Eric said "I made my way back to the crew as they were starting to leave the bar. I fell in step and we arrived at the hotel."

"Cliff said, 'Eric, you can take room 107 - that's my room. I'll bunk in with Frog tonight. See you downstairs in the dining room for breakfast at seven in the morning. Welcome aboard, son.' "

"I slept well. The bed was heavenly compared to where I'd been sleeping for the past two years. I was up at six. I showered and went down stairs to the dining room. Frog and Cliff were already there and having coffee."

" 'Good morning Eric. How'd you sleep last night?'

"Well, thanks, and I want to thank you for hiring me on your crew. I hope I can do a good job. I'm a hard worker and I'll do my best."

" 'I'm sure you will, son. Now dig into those pancakes. You'll need a good breakfast under your belt for this loading job today.' "

Eric paused to take a swallow and then began again. "We got busy after breakfast. Frog took me under his wing and taught me how to break down the equipment and load it for traveling to the next location. We were headed to Yuma, which wasn't that far from San Diego. Their next movie was about drug trafficking. How ironic was that! The movie would have a lot of English and Spanish speaking people playing the parts, so Cliff's crew needed to be able to communicate with the actors. Frog told me, right from the get go, that keeping the actors happy was part of our job. Their wishes were the most important and that when they asked for something, it was up to us to keep them satisfied."

"Cliff found me and asked me where I was born. 'I need to send for your birth certificate so we can get you a passport. Do you remember the name of the county?'"

" 'I know it was Clark County in Holbrook, Wisconsin.' I replied."

" 'I'll get this paperwork completed and sent out in today's mail. I've been watching you, Eric, and I can see that you are learning the correct way to go about breaking down the cables and lights,' Cliff said. 'Frog is the best man on the job at showing new hires how to go about things.' "

"You know, I was lucky to have been in that bar at the right place at the right time. Cliff and Frog were upright men. I not only had made two new lifelong friends but was learning a trade and would always be able to get a job."

Eric looked around at his audience and asked, "Are any of you ready to hit the sack? I can stop anytime and continue tomorrow."

"Son, we're riveted to find out what you've been doing the past thirty years. We can sleep in tomorrow."

"Well, after going to Yuma, Arizona for about six weeks it was time to go overseas. My passport had arrived and I was given my shots before I went abroad. We headed for Hong Kong. This was a big step for me and a chance to see the world. What an education and what an adventure. I loved my job and knew I wouldn't always be the cable and lights guy. Cliff hinted that he could see me moving up the ladder in the company and taking on more responsibility. I was open for that opportunity and continued to advance. One night I overheard Frog and Cliff talking about me. 'Do you think Eric is ready for Steve's job?' Cliff asked."

"I knew Steve was going to be promoted to a foreman's job. He was in charge of a lot of detailed work and answered directly to Cliff. Frog said 'Let's see how he handles the Hong Kong move. If all goes well and we have no serious problems, I'm ready to give Eric more responsibility. He can have the advancement when we give Steve his promotion.' "

"I was content to wait my turn and knew I would be grateful when and if it happened. I'd put in less than six months with the company but I knew I'd do well if I continued to do my job to the best of my ability. No more jail time for me. I'd learned a tough lesson in that Tijuana hellhole of the world and didn't intend to ever go that route again. I had a brain and intended to use it. So far no one I worked with knew I'd been in jail, but in the back of my mind I had thoughts that maybe Cliff knew it from that first day we'd met in the bar. But since it wasn't mentioned I sure as hell wasn't going to bring it up. Let that chapter in my life be dead and hopefully forgotten forever."

He added, "These apples with caramel sauce are delicious, Mom."

"I remembered you used to like them," I grinned.

"So you've had an interesting life traveling all over the world. You must get that from me," I said. "I think both of you boys like the moving around to new places kind of life. Kent, you did it in the service for twenty years. Do you miss it now that you're settled in Phoenix?"

"Not really, Mom. I like being settled in one place now that I'm nearing fifty. Traveling takes a lot out of you, but I enjoyed it in my younger years. Marianne is a swell gal and we've talked of getting married. She has a grown daughter, Vivian, from her first marriage, and a ten year old grandson Jordan. They live in Phoenix so they have become my extended family. The two of us are planning to tie the knot this year. Maybe we can make it a family reunion around that celebration. We'll give everybody plenty of notice so they can all attend."

"That sounds terrific, Son. This is wonderful being reunited with the two of you tonight. I don't want to even think of the years we spent apart. We'll look forward to our future and the happiness it will bring to all of us."

Eric said "I think I will be able to retire at the age of sixty. Cliff has taken me into his family like a son and I think of him as the dad I never knew. I have paid my dues, so to speak, at work, and have advanced over the years. I became a part owner after I'd been with the company five years. I am currently in charge of a work crew and still do a lot of paper work for Cliff. He is about to retire, so I may be promoted to his position. I know it backward and forward now and I think he'll turn over the reins to me when that happens. I knew that the movie making business was always going to be around, and investing in it was my way of setting up my retirement. Unfortunately traveling did not give me the choice of having a wife and family, but I've been rewarded in other ways.

"I currently have a long time girl friend, Gloria, who doesn't mind my long absences. She is a buyer for Macy's Department Store and does a lot of traveling herself. Both of us have a good understanding of what it takes to be in the businesses we're in, thus we really do appreciate our time together. She's based out of Chicago so that's why I'm there when I'm not on location."

I spoke up. "Well, I can see we're all tired and fighting sleep, why don't we call it a night? We can talk more tomorrow before you boys head back to Phoenix. Since it's so late, Karen, why don't you stay here too? You can bunk in with me. My second bedroom has twin beds and I think you boys will be comfortable in there."

"This has been such a big relief for me to get caught up on the past so we can go on into the future." Eric said. "Come on, little brother, let's hit the sack."

Karen and I were up early the next morning and having coffee in the kitchen when we heard Kent coming down the hallway. "Good morning, Son. How did you sleep?" I asked.

"Just fine, Mom. Good mattresses you have on those beds. Eric is just now getting up. I'll have a cup of that java. It sure smells good."

"I've got lots of it made and I'll start some bacon now that you boys are up and hungry. Do you still like your eggs sunny side up?"

"You remembered." Kent smiled, obviously pleased. "Yes, I do."

Just then Eric appeared in the kitchen doorway. "That smells like good coffee, Mom. I need it after talking my throat dry last night. Sure hope I didn't bore all of you with my endless chatter."

"We all found your story fascinating and now we know why we didn't hear from you. Just knowing that you have had a career in the movie making business and that you like what you do makes me very happy, Son," I replied.

"Kent, tell us about your career in the service and then on to what you are doing now with computers." Karen asked.

"I learned a lot about computers in the military and when I finished my twenty years with the Marines I continued to like the challenge of fixing them. That's what I do now and it's an easy job with good pay. I can't think of anything I'd rather be doing at this time in my life. I have a few good buddies that I keep in touch with and we have a reunion once a year. Steve from high school and I have had some real hair-raising experiences. We are still good friends and probably always will be. He's married; his wife's name is Brenda and they have three kids. They currently live in Oklahoma City but Steve is talking of moving to Las Vegas where Brenda's folks live. They want her parents to be able to see and enjoy their grandchildren more.

Steve owns his own electronics business and can relocate there."

I'd been making the bacon and eggs while Karen fixed the toast. I made another pot of coffee and said, "its eating time, fellows. Let's dig in. I'm sure you're good and hungry by now. I know I am."

We sat down and enjoyed our breakfast. I thought to myself that this was a moment to savor as I had had many dreams and sleepless nights when I never thought it would happen. I did not want it to end.

When we finally finished breakfast and the second pot of coffee, I asked "Do you boys have any points of interest that you'd like to see in Tucson while you're here? I'd be happy to drive you around. I make a good tour guide."

"I'd just like to relax here and visit with you and Aunt Karen, if that's ok with all of you. What time is it getting to be? I need to catch my flight back to Chicago at seven tonight. What time do we need to leave Tucson to get back to the Phoenix airport, Kent?"

"If we leave here by two thirty or three this afternoon we will make it on time. It's noon now, so we'll get out of the kitchen, unless you need some help, Mom. Let's see if there's some football on TV, Eric."

"Karen and I can handle the KP duties. You and Eric enjoy yourselves in the family room."

When we finished in the kitchen, I decided to get out some old photo albums for the boys to see. But they were interested in the football game, so I put them aside. There'd be another time when we could look at old photographs. It warmed my heart to see the two of them laughing and enjoying the game together. I was a very proud mom to see that my sons had turned out to be fine young men.

"I think I'll head on home and do a few chores around the house for the rest of the afternoon," Karen said. "It sure has been a wonderful reunion and I'll look forward to many more with you fellows." The boys got up and embraced Karen in a three way hug.

After she left I sat down with my sons and watched the football game with them.

When it was over I talked about Grandpa and Grandma Fuller's, Aunt Clara's and my Dad's passing. Kent knew but Eric of course did not. I did not mention that I had attended only Grandpa Fuller's funeral. This was a happy time in the house and I wanted to keep it that way.

Too soon it was time to for them to gather up their belongings and hit the road for Phoenix. The three of us hugged for a long time. "You two have made me the happiest mother in the world." I said.

"On your ride back to Phoenix, Kent, you can tell Eric how I encouraged you to make a life on your own after graduation."

"Mom, that was the best thing you could have done. I just didn't know it at the time. Picking up my mattress and sliding it half off the bed got my attention all right. It got me moving in the right direction and into the Marines. Over the years, they made a man out of me," he laughed.

"They did a good job of it, too. I'm proud of both you boys. Many times when you were growing up I didn't think you were listening to me or what I was telling you, but I can see it all turned out well. Drive safe and keep in touch. I love you guys."

"We love you too. Stay well and happy until we meet again. I'll coordinate our wedding around a family reunion and we'll make it this year sometime." Kent said.

I stayed in the driveway watching them disappear from view. Years of worrying and wondering about Eric were behind me now.

CHAPTER 28

I called Karen and told her the boys had just left for Phoenix. "I feel such peace in my heart at this moment that it's unbelievable. I'm so thankful to be all together as a family. Being reunited with both of them is such a blessing; I never believed it would happen." I knew I'd sleep well that night with pleasant dreams.

Karen and I continued to have our Saturday morning coffee chats. I asked her one morning, "How did you manage to keep your marriage together for thirty years?"

She replied "I can't say that I knowingly did anything terrific. I did have a deep emotional commitment to Junior right from the beginning. We were in love and our feelings grew stronger as we worked through the ebb and flow of our marriage. We managed to stick together through the good times and bad. I think he put my feelings first in his heart and I did the same with him. He was a sensitive husband which is exactly what I needed to stay true to him. I respected him and the way he provided for the family. Who knows, maybe if I'd seen that he was restless after the kids were grown, I could have helped him rekindle our earlier love. But by the time I was aware of his feelings, he was already looking for wife number two and it was too late to save the marriage."

I said "I guess I started out most of my marriages without a good foundation and didn't really know what to look for in a man's character. I relied on my quick instincts of how they looked or the pickup lines they fed me. I had no respect for Dad, so my memories of him were no help to me when I started looking for a husband. I wanted to be in love … I felt I had a right to be in love. I expected marriage to foster and grow those deep feelings that I was looking for. Falling in love was easy, but staying in love is what I had no answers for. Maybe without much of a courtship, I didn't know how to invite warm cherished feelings. I had strong feelings regarding sex, but I needed to learn the art of romance. When all that was absent I became quickly convinced that divorce was justifiable."

Karen nodded. "I know you had true love in your marriage with Bud. The five years you had together with him were what every woman dreams about. So you know that it can happen. The rest of your choices were probably made too hastily without really any courtship. You have to admit that your career has been one of the most important things in your life and some of those husbands just couldn't handle that. But it happened, and now you've put it past you and moved on with your life. I'm proud of you."

"Thanks, Karen. I needed that pep talk."

Karen continued to sum up her current outlook on life. "I know you're content now to be without a man for the rest of your life and that's your choice. I, on the other hand, still think I'll find somebody that will want to love and cherish me for who I am. We've both walked a rocky road and hopefully learned from our experiences. The future is whatever we make of it. I'm happier now than I've been in a long time and I can see that you are, too."

I said "We're in this together, until the end, Karen. I've got your back and you've got mine on this last leg of our journey through life."

She nodded, smiling.

"I think we can call ourselves *true survivors*."

Made in the USA
Middletown, DE
29 September 2021